Vue de la Ville de Moscou prise de la gauche du Balcon du Palais Imperial

Cette vue & la précédente sont les plus belles de la Collection. On les doit à l'empressement que Sa
Majesté Paul Premier fit paroitre de les avoir en peinture. On y découvre une partie de l'enceinte
du Kremlin, tout ce qui est de la ville sous ce point de vue & tout ce qui s'étend au dela
Entrepris aux frais de Jean Walser, Peignant de la premiere Classe à Moscou publié
en 1799 avec Privilege de Sa Majesté Imperiale Paul Premier Empereur
de toutes les Russies.

MOSCOW

GREAT CENTERS OF ART

MOSCOW

Edited by Valeri S. Turchin

ALLANHELD & SCHRAM
MONTCLAIR

GEORGE PRIOR
LONDON

Translated from the German by Barbara Beedham

2246

© 1981 Edition Leipzig

Published in the United States of America in 1981
by Abner Schram Ltd., 36 Park Street,
Montclair, N. J. 07042
and Allanheld, Osmun & Co.,
19 Brunswick Road, Montclair, N. J. 07042

Published in the United Kingdom in 1981
by George Prior Associated Publishers Ltd.
37–41 Bedford Row, London WC1R 4JH
ENGLAND
ISBN: 0 86043 502 4

Library of Congress Catalog Card Number: 80-666 51
ISBN: 0 8390-0255-6

Front inside cover: View of Moscow from the left side of the
terrace at the tsar's palace.
Back inside cover: View of the Kremlin and its surrounding
area in Moscow.
Both from: Guerard de la Barthe,
Pictorial views of Moscow 1794–1797

Designed by Horst Erich Wolter and Herbert Eckardt
Printed in the German Democratic Republic

This work, a joint project of Moscow art experts, was edited by Valeri S. Turchin,
who also wrote three of the background articles.
The other contributors are Yuri M. Ovsyannikov and Natalya Y. Semyonova.

Articles:

Moscow as a city of art	V. S. Turchin
The Tretyakov Gallery	V. S. Turchin
The Pushkin Fine Arts Museum	N. Y. Semyonova
Museums of the Moscow Kremlin	Y. M. Ovsyannikov
Andrei Rublyov Museum of Ancient Russian Art	Y. M. Ovsyannikov
Historic estates	V. S. Turchin

CONTENTS

MOSCOW AS A CITY OF ART

Countless art treasures have been accumulated within Moscow's walls over the past eight hundred years. Initially, collecting was sporadic, random, and disorganized, but in time the acquisition of art works became systematized. Foreign and native masters, covering the full range of artistic endeavors over the centuries, are represented in the Moscow collections. Reserved in the past for a privileged few, they are in our time open to the public, bringing pleasure to millions of visitors and providing information on the most important periods and styles in art.

The original centers for art in ancient Russia were primarily cathedrals, churches, and monasteries. Handmade liturgical objects were valued as artistic treasures as well as implements of religious worship. Thus the sacristies in a sense housed the first art collections. A large number of valuable icons, the hallmarks of Russian religious art, were brought to Moscow, by then the focal point of a rapidly developing area of northeastern Russia. After the Moscow School of Painting was founded in the sixteenth century, churches and cathedrals in the city were richly decorated by contemporary masters, enhancing Moscow's role as a center of religious art.

By the sixteenth century, lay connoisseurs emerged from the city's aristocracy, and skilled artisans and masters were kept busy in the Kremlin's workshops. The first royal collections, made up of stocks of weapons and household goods, were kept in the Armory. As time went on, the Armory lost the function of art workshop and increasingly became a storehouse, the place where the royal treasures were kept. As Moscow's administrative and economic strength grew in the sixteenth century, so did the size of the royal collections. At the same time, the first collections of weapons and household articles appeared in the castles of the boyars.

In the seventeenth century, more attention was paid to collecting systematically. The reforms of Peter I initiated a new epoch for Russia, and this was reflected in Moscow's art collections. St. Petersburg (now Leningrad) became the capital, but Moscow retained its importance as the economic and cultural center of the country.

Peter I is considered the founder of the first museums in both cities. In 1698, he returned to Russia with a collection of rare objects from countries of Western Europe and set up an art chamber in Moscow (later administered by the Academy of Sciences). In 1720, Peter I chose the Armory as the site of a permanent collection of antiquities and curios—the first museum to unite Russian art treasures in painting and sculpture with artifacts of the decorative arts. During the reign of Peter I, private collections were established in increasing numbers. Libraries and small galleries for paintings, sculptures, and curios were set up in the homes of the aristocracy.

A characteristic feature of this period was the construction of country residences in the area surrounding Moscow. On these large country estates, as in their city palaces, the nobles surrounded themselves with splendid art treasures. Among the summer residences built in the eighteenth century by wealthy aristocrats were Kuskovo, Arkhangelskoye, and Ostankino.

At that time collectors were particularly interested in the art of Western Europe, especially France and Italy. The works of native masters were only an adjunct.

The nineteenth century was of great significance for Moscow collections. In 1810 a new building for the tsar's Armory treasures was completed. Unique works of art from the cathedrals of the Moscow

7

Kremlin were stored there. But the city did not yet have a public art museum, and in the mid nineteenth century, educated Muscovites expressed strong sentiments for one. Interest in Russian art was growing, and the range of collections widened. The nobility's collections, housed in palaces and on country estates away from public viewing, decreased in importance as merchants and scholars devoted themselves more and more to serious collecting. Special collections on specific themes came into being, with preference shown for old Dutch and German masters and ancient Russian art.

The growing interest in antiquities can be explained largely by the development of scientific methodology and national awareness, the latter heightened by the War of 1812. Illustrative of this interest are the valuable collections of Russian art made by K. T. Soldatenkov and F. I. Pryanishnikov (both originally of St. Petersburg) in the early nineteenth century.

Despite the mushrooming of private collections in Moscow, pressure to obtain a state museum was not successful until 1862 when the Rumyantsev Museum with its comprehensive library was donated to the city of Moscow. The Rumyantsev Museum was founded in 1831 in St. Petersburg. With its many books, rare manuscripts, and maps, it became the heart of what is now the Lenin Library, one of the world's largest collections. Pryanishnikov's collection and examples of Western European art from the Hermitage (founded by Catherine II in St. Petersburg) were later added to the original collection.

P. M. Tretyakov founded a museum of national art, an act of major significance for Moscow, indeed for the whole of Russia. Together, the Rumyantsev Museum and the Tretyakov Gallery held the largest collections of national and Western European art in pre-Soviet Moscow.

At the turn of the century, extensive collections of modern Western European art were set up by S. I. Shchukin and I. A. Morozov. Experts found their artistic standard to be high—equal to the major museums of Paris and other Western capitals. Valuable collections were also assembled in the early 1900s by wealthy merchants and members of the upper-middle classes. Included were works by early Western European masters, contemporary Russian painters, and masters of old Russia who had been neglected for a long time.

In 1912, the Museum of Fine Arts, containing magnificent examples of sculpture from private collections, was opened in Moscow.

Some of the museums of the day could barely survive. The government granted them only meager financial aid, insufficient to make new acquisitions. Private collectors, on the other hand, continued to acquire new works, but these purchases reflected the taste and preferences of individuals, and were not made in accordance with any objective criteria or plan. Furthermore, these collections were often inaccessible to the public at large.

The situation changed after the 1917 Revolution. The young republic directed its attention to the Russian art scene and nationalized museums and private collections. On September 19, 1918, a decree forbidding the export of art works was issued by the people's commissars. On October 5, a regulation was published on the registration and protection of art treasures and antiquities owned by private individuals, societies, and institutions. In Moscow the Central State Museum Fund became very active. Scientists traveled across the country to locate and protect works of art. Exhibitions of new acquisitions were held frequently.

In the first few years of Soviet rule, Moscow's art collections were greatly expanded. What was once scattered throughout the city and surrounding areas was now brought together, forming collections of considerable value. The department for museums and the preservation of monuments, attached to the Commissariat for Education, classified the art works carefully, thus creating the basis for the present-day Moscow museums.

The 1920s, then, saw formation of the leading museum collections in Moscow. They have since been further expanded, and will continue to grow.

Today there are 63 museums in Moscow. The largest art museums in the city are the Tretyakov Gallery, the Pushkin Fine Arts Museum, the museums of the Kremlin, and the Andrei Rublyov Museum of Ancient Russian Art. There are interesting collections at Kuskovo, Arkhangelskoye, and Ostankino. Moscow also abounds in small museums like those set up in the former studios of Russian painters like Tropinin, Golubkina, Konenkov, and Korin, and the Shchusev Museum for the History of Architecture provides a wide-ranging exhibition of material on both ancient and modern buildings.

THE TRETYAKOV GALLERY

The existence of the Tretyakov Gallery and its magnificent collections is due entirely to one man, Pavel Mikhailovich Tretyakov (1832–1898). A wealthy merchant and, like many members of his class in the mid nineteenth century, an enthusiastic art collector, Tretyakov brought a special vision and passion to his collecting activities. He began with the purchase of a number of engravings by old Italian masters but soon devoted himself to the work of Russian painters. *The temptation* by N. G. Shilder and *Encounter with smugglers* by V. G. Khudyakov—both graduates of the Moscow School of Painting—were bought in 1856, laying the foundation for Tretyakov's famous collection of paintings by Russian artists.

Toward the end of the 1850s and throughout the 1860s, many paintings from neglected collections of the Russian nobility were sold at auctions in Moscow and St. Petersburg. Tretyakov succeeded in acquiring some works from V. A. Kokoryev's collection.

About this time the outstanding collection of F. I. Pryanishnikov (1793–1867), the recently deceased director of postal services, came up for sale in St. Petersburg. One of the richest collections of Russian painting in existence, it comprised 84 works. The very high price demanded for the collection, however, prevented Tretyakov from buying it. In the end, the state bought the collection and turned it over to the Rumyantsev Museum. Far from discouraging Tretyakov, this course of events only strengthened his determination to collect works of the Russian school. Tretyakov's primary aim now was to create, entirely through his own efforts, a museum of national art. By the 1860s he already owned paintings from the early nineteenth century, for example, *The great harbor in Sorrento* by S. F. Shchedrin, *Portrait of the archeologist, M. A. Lanchi* by K. P. Bryullov, *Princess Tarakanova* by K. D. Flavitsky, and *The market* by N. A. Nevrev, as well as portraits by A. P. Antropov, F. S. Rokotov, and D. G. Levitsky. In 1861, Tretyakov bought paintings by contemporary artists, including *The prisoners resting* by V. I. Yakoby and *Village procession at Easter* by V. G. Perov (which, however, censors removed from the collection).

In 1870, the Society of Traveling Art Exhibitions was founded in St. Petersburg. Its members wanted to break away from academic art and present their work to broader segments of the population. From 1871 on, the society held annual exhibitions, first in St. Petersburg and Moscow and later in many other Russian towns. Tretyakov became a follower and supporter of the "Wanderers," as the members of the society were then called. He acquired paintings for his collection from their exhibitions. The best works of the society's masters, I. N. Kramskoi, G. G. Myassoyedov, N. N. Ghe, Perov, I. Y. Repin, V. I. Surikov, V. Y. Makovsky, A. K. Savrassov, I. I. Shishkin, A. I. Kuindzhy, N. A. Yaroshenko, I. I. Levitan, and V. A. Serov decorated Tretyakov's gallery, depicting in full the aims and development of the "Wanderers" and their movement.

In the 1870s, Russia experienced a rapid advance in science, literature, and art. This reinforced Tretyakov's desire, as expressed by Repin, to capture the "beloved faces of the nation." The first painter who produced portraits especially for the gallery was Perov. He was soon followed by Kramskoi, Ghe, and Repin.

All the paintings in P. M. Tretyakov's collection were kept at his home in Lavrushinsky Lane, where the Tretyakov family had settled in 1851. As the collection grew, it soon became apparent that more space would be needed. In 1872, work was begun on a picture gallery adjoining the south side of the house. In 1874, the pictures were placed in the new rooms.

In 1882, after purchasing the Turkestan series by V. V. Vereshchagin (Tretyakov had about 150 works in all by this artist), another extension was needed. Six new halls were now available for works by Vereshchagin and Russian artists of the latter half of the eighteenth century and the beginning of the nineteenth century. Prints collected by Tretyakov from the 1880s, were placed on exhibition in one of the halls. In order to display the art works more effectively, Tretyakov in 1879 had the windows of his house walled in and a glass roof fitted to provide more favorable lighting.

Beginning in 1874, after the two extensions were built, Tretyakov opened his collection to some visitors from the general public, and in 1881 the "Tretyakovka," as the gallery was then called, opened its doors to the public at large. A private collection was in this way transformed into a museum accessible, free of charge, to all art lovers. The Hermitage and the Academy of Arts in St. Petersburg and the Rumyantsev Museum in Moscow also had sections on Russian art, but access was limited to the aristocracy. In contrast, people of all classes went to the Tretyakovka. Soon, visiting the gallery came to be regarded as a must, and as early as 1890 it was widely recognized as the preeminent museum of Russian national art.

As the years progressed, lack of space made itself increasingly evident. Paintings covered the walls from ceiling to floor, which made it difficult to study them properly. In 1885, a new extension provided another seven halls in which works by Repin (the collection of his paintings totaled fifty), Surikov, and V. D. Polyonov were displayed. In 1892, a fourth extension added another five halls.

Tretyakov's younger brother, S. M. Tretyakov, died on June 25, 1892, leaving half of his house in Lavrushinsky Lane and a handsome sum of money to the city of Moscow, but his collection of paintings by foreign masters went to his brother. This act was probably instrumental in P. M. Tretyakov's decision to present his gallery to the city. On August 31, 1892, Tretyakov handed the city council a declaration assigning to the city of Moscow his whole collection and that of his brother—a total of about two thousand paintings. On August 15, 1893, after the Moscow city council had confirmed its acceptance of the gallery, it was officially reopened to the public. A dream long cherished by Russian intellectuals—a

publicly owned museum of national art accessible to all—was fulfilled.

Tsar Alexander III's reaction to this event was: "The Muscovite merchant has gotten in ahead of the ruler!" And indeed a second museum of national art—the Russian Museum in St. Petersburg—was not completed until 1897, when paintings by Russian artists were transferred to the Mikhailov Palace from two halls in the Hermitage and from the Museum of the Academy of Arts.

In 1894, the Moscow Society of Art Lovers called the first conference of Russian artists. Held at the Tretyakov Gallery, it led numerous artists to present their own works to the gallery; other people donated works of Russian art they purchased or inherited.

In 1897–98 the last extension to the gallery was made—a one-story building with two halls in which S. M. Tretyakov's collection of Western European painting was installed.

In 1898, P. M. Tretyakov died, his wife four months later. The Tretyakovs' private apartments ceased to exist. The main entrance to the house and the façade were redesigned by the artist, V. M. Vasnetsov, and by 1902 the building reflected the picturesque style of popular Russian architecture. The new façade was embellished with Moscow's coat of arms—portraying St. George killing the dragon with his lance—and bore the inscription: "Moscow City Art Gallery dedicated to Pavel Mikhailovich and Sergei Mikhailovich Tretyakov. Founded by P. M. Tretyakov in 1856 and presented by him to the city of Moscow together with the collection of S. M. Tretyakov."

After P. M. Tretyakov's death, the gallery was administered by a council created specifically for this purpose and chaired by the mayor of Moscow. The first council included the artists, V. A. Serov and I. S. Ostroukhov, as well as representatives of the Moscow city council. In 1905, Ostroukhov, a distinguished artist and collector, was made director of the gallery. He contributed to its development by the addition of old Russian icons and the purchase of paintings by old masters of the eighteenth century.

In 1913, the painter and art historian, I. E. Grabar, took over from Ostroukhov and administered the gallery until 1925. He was responsible for classifying the collection scientifically and publishing a complete catalogue. (Catalogues of acquisitions and exhibitions had appeared annually from 1893). Grabar also instituted the policy of hanging the art works chronologically in the individual halls.

Donations to the gallery continued. In 1910, M. K. Morozova presented part of the collection of her husband, M. A. Morozov, best known as a collector of modern French painting. The Russian section was enriched with paintings by Serov and M. A. Vrubel.

On July 3, 1918, V. I. Lenin signed a decree nationalizing the Tretyakov Gallery. This led to a large-scale expansion of the gallery through the addition of treasures from private collections, monasteries, and churches. In 1925, the largest collection of Russian painting, consisting of various individual collections, was received from the former Rumyantsev Museum. Included were A. A. Ivanov's famous painting, *The appearance of Christ to the people*, and a large number of studies and sketches. In 1932, a new hall was added to the Tretyakov Gallery to provide room for the display of these works.

The items from the Rumyantsev Museum included Pryanishnikov's collection, which Tretyakov had once tried to acquire. Among these acquisitions were such important works as *A new cavalier* and *The major in debt out courting* by P. A. Fedotov, *Man reading a newspaper* by O. A. Kiprensky, *The lace maker* by V. A. Tropinin and *Self-portrait in an armchair* by K. P. Bryullov.

In addition to the 172 paintings by 84 Russian masters in the Pryanishnikov collection, the items transferred to the Tretyakov Gallery from the former Rumyantsev Museum included about 230 works by Russian artists assembled by yet another great collector of Russian art, the publisher, K. T. Soldatenkov.

The nationalization of several more private collections (for example, V. O. Girshman's) raised the level of Russian art exhibited publicly far beyond that available at the beginning of the twentieth century. Many interesting examples of Russian sculpture were also added to the gallery when old collections belonging to the aristocracy were put up for sale. Acquisitions to the sculpture section increased markedly when the sculptor, V. N. Domogatsky, was director of the sculpture section.

In 1925, the Tsvetkov Gallery, which had been established in the 1880s by the banker, I. E. Tsvetkov (1845–1917), was incorporated into the Tretyakov Gallery. In 1909, Tsvetkov, in a gesture that had become traditional among Russian collectors, had donated his collection to the city of Moscow. It contained over three hundred paintings and twelve hundred drawings, including works by Levitsky, Kiprensky, A. G. Venetsianov, Tropinin, and Fedotov.

Through exchanges with the Russian Museum of Leningrad, the Tretyakov Gallery received several first-class works, among them the *Portrait of P. N. Demidov* by Levitsky.

The Tretyakov Gallery in 1925 held an exhibition on "150 years of Russian art." This was a huge success and bestowed even greater prestige on the Tretyakovka.

In 1929, the gallery received the Ostroukhov collection, comprising important works of ancient art, especially by Russian masters. With this collection, the Museum of Icons and Paintings was founded in 1918 as a branch of the Tretyakov Gallery. The icons collected by Tretyakov and Ostroukhov formed the nucleus of the now extensive section on ancient Russian art. In 1930, it was expanded by transfer of the collection of icons that had been placed in the Museum of History in 1926.

The Tretyakov Gallery's sculpture collection has also grown. It, too, received articles from the Museum of History (for example, the bust of F. I. Shubin), and over the years it has acquired works by such famous Russian sculptors as Golubkina, Konenkov, and N. A. Andreyev.

Numerous acquisitions have been made with the aid of the state commission for art. Besides works by old Russian masters, paintings by contemporary artists have been bought for the section on Soviet art, which was established in the 1930s. Works of this nature were acquired at exhibitions, directly from the artists, from private collections, and abroad. The directors of the museum encouraged the acquisition of self-portraits, and also collected iconographic material, together with designs, studies, and sketches.

The museum exhibited actively and extensively. The work of the Tretyakov Gallery was regarded as an essential element in the development of socialist culture, and great attention was paid to the widespread propagation of Russian and Soviet art. During the Second World War the treasures of the Tretyakov Gallery were taken to the country for safety. Artistic life, however, did not stop in the halls of the museum; exhibitions of individual masters and of modern art on particular themes were held regularly.

At present the general expansion of all the museum's sections is continuing. The collection of Soviet painting, sculpture, and graphic arts is growing steadily. The inventory of ancient Russian art is also being enlarged. Every year, staff scientists scour individual areas of the country for new art treasures. The icon collection in the Tretyakov Gallery is the largest in the Soviet Union, comprising about four thousand works, for which a complete scientific catalogue has been published. Various trends in ancient Russian art are represented here, such as the schools of Kiev-Rus, Novgorod, Pskov, Moscow, Tver, and Rostov-Suzdal. The works by Theophanes the Greek, a Byzantine emigrant from Constantinople, and Andrei Rublyov, one of his immediate followers, are of world repute. The style of ancient Russian painting which developed between the eleventh and seventeenth centuries is fascinating in the diversity of its forms and figures. Religious asceticism and worldliness stand side by side; Byzantine severity joins popular, folklore elements.

The precise skill of this painting, based on a combination of finely modeled areas and expressive lines, appears modern even today. When Matisse came to Russia in 1911, he was impressed by the wholeness and harmony of the figures of ancient Russian masters.

Today, each section of the Tretyakov Gallery has its own particular character. The first attempts at worldly art in Russia, which were linked with Tsar Peter I's reforms, can be seen in the form of portraits and sculptures in the collection of eighteenth-century Russian art. Portraiture was the culmination of Russian painting in the eighteenth century, as the Enlightenment strove to discover the individual features of man. This is exemplified in the fine work of Antropov, Rokotov, Levitsky, and F. I. Shubin. Romanticism is represented in the work of Kiprensky and Bryullov. At the beginning of the nineteenth century, Russian landscape painting, hitherto limited mainly to decorative panels on palace walls, gained in importance. In this field of art, the name S. F. Shchedrin deserves special mention. The Russian Biedermeier period is represented in works by Tropinin, Fedotov, and A. G. Venetsianov and many of his pupils.

The first of the realist painters was Perov with his portraits and genre scenes. He was succeeded by the generation of the "Wanderers," whose basic aims—criticism of society and revolutionary ideals—considerably influenced Russian art in the second half of the nineteenth century. Naturalist trends also appeared at this time in landscape painting (Savrassov) and in historical painting (Vereshchagin). The mournfulness of people lost in thought is incorporated in the figures of Kramskoi, while the captivating feature of Repin's work is the broad nature of the theme and its closeness to life. For Russian culture, then, the nineteenth century was a time of coherent artistic trends and abundant talent.

At the turn of the century, various styles superseded each other in rapid succession, starting with Impressionism (Serov) and finishing with Expressionism and Cubism (the "Knave of Diamonds" group of artists and the work of Chagall).

Soviet art in the Tretyakov Gallery is worthy of special attention. Artists like P. V. Kuznetsov, M. S. Zaryan, K. S. Petrov-Vodkin, I. I. Mashkov, A. A. Rylov, K. F. Yuon, P. P. Konchalovski, K. N. Istomin, and D. P. Sterenberg led the way. In the thirties they were followed chiefly by B. V. Yoganzon, M. V. Nesterov, Y. I. Pimenov, S. V. Gerassimov, A. A. Deineka, and V. I. Mukhina. The last halls of the section on Soviet painting are reserved for masters of the postwar years and of the present. Much emphasis is placed on the work of artists from the various Soviet republics.

In the early 1980s, the Tretyakov Gallery, already one of the largest art museums in the Soviet Union, will transfer some of its exhibits to a new building, now nearing completion. The displays in the new gallery will concentrate on the achievements of the peoples of the USSR.

The Tretyakov Gallery is also a research institute of repute. It directs search and discovery, establishes the provenance of individual works of art, authenticates them, is responsible for the preservation and restoration of art treasures, and publishes numerous art catalogues. A library and archives of photographs and manuscripts are also ·part of the museum.

Lectures and scientific conferences, often combined with special exhibitions, are held regularly in the gallery. There is a club for young art lovers. Illustrated books, reproductions, and television programs give the art treasures of the Tretyakov Gallery a wide audience.

In the last few decades the gallery has participated increasingly in activities outside its walls. It has taken part in exhibitions throughout the Soviet Union and in countless international exhibitions. Works of art from the Tretyakov Gallery have appeared at exhibitions in Poland, Hungary, the German Democratic Republic, Czechoslovakia, Austria, Italy, France, the United States, Mexico, Japan, and Sweden.

Together with the Russian Museum in Leningrad, the Tretyakov Gallery illustrates the development of Russian and Soviet art from its origins to the present day.

NOTES ON ILLUSTRATIONS

1 *Trinity*, 1422–1427. Andrei Rublyov (about 1370–1430). Egg tempera on wood, 142×114 cm. Acquired in 1929 from the Museum of History and Art in Zagorsk. Layers of overpainting were removed from the icon in 1905 and again in 1918–19. Rublyov painted the *Trinity* at the request of Patriarch Nikon as a memorial to Sergei of Radonezh, the founder in the 15th century of the Trinity Monastery of St. Sergius in modern-day Zagorsk. God appears to old Abraham and his wife, Sarah, in the form of the three wanderers, the angels asking for shelter. The angels are sitting on thrones around a table bearing a dish containing the sacrificed lamb. The building, tree, and mountain in the upper part of the icon are symbols of the development of the world, of life, and of the strength of the spirit. Bright colors and lightly rounded lines are typical of Rublyov's style.

2 *Our Lady of Vladimir*, early 12th century. Constantinople school. Egg tempera on wood, original size 78×55 cm, later enlarged to 100×70 cm. Acquired in 1930 from the Museum of History; originally brought to Kiev from Constantinople around 1136, transferred to Vladimir in 1155 by Andrei Bogolyubski, moved again in 1395 to the Cathedral of the Assumption in the Moscow Kremlin, and placed in the Museum of History. Of the original painting only the face of the Virgin Mary and that of the child have survived. The icon was painted over repeatedly, and these layers were not removed until 1918. It embodies the widespread iconographic theme of "Our Lady of Tenderness," where the Christ child nestles against his mother's cheek. This painting served as the model for countless works by Russian masters.

3 *Demetrius of Solun*, about 1113. Russian and Byzantine artists of the Constantinople school. Mosaic with lime background, smalt, colored stones, marble, 222×129 cm. Acquired in 1938 from the Kiev Museum of Russian Art. This mosaic was originally situated at the southern edge of the northeastern pillar under the east arch of the nave in St. Michael's Church in Kiev. It is regarded as the oldest example of mosaic work in ancient Russian art. The figure of the saint is depicted from the front. He holds a spear and a shield in his hands. His name is written in Greek letters to the left and right of his head.

4 *Crucifixion*, 1500. Dionisi (mid 15th century to early 16th century). Egg tempera on wood, 85×52 cm. Acquired from the iconostasis of the Trinity Cathedral of the Pavlovo–Obnorsk Monastery. The *Crucifixion* is a late work by Dionisi. His original style is illustrated by the striking elongation of the figures and the particularly subtle coloring.

5 *Madonna in the garden*, about 1670. Nikita Pavlovets (died 1677/78). Fabric on wood, 33×29 cm. Acquired in 1940; originally in Shcherbatov family collection. N. Pavlovets was a serf of Prince Cherkaski. In 1959 the icon was cleaned and layers of overpainting removed. In the center stands the Virgin Mary, being crowned by two angels. She is in a garden, the age-old view of paradise. The painting was probably influenced iconographically by Western European etchings.

6 *The miracle of Flor and Laurentius*, last quarter of the 15th century. Novgorod school. Egg distemper on wood, 67×52 cm. Acquired in 1930 from the Moscow Museum of History; originally in A. V. Morozov collection. The cult of Flor and Laurentius arose among peasants and horse breeders. According to legend, these saints were chosen by Michael the Archangel to guard herds of horses against losses. In Slav and Russian literature, the brothers Flor and Laurentius are Christian martyrs who had worked as builders. The icon depicts the scene of Michael the Archangel placing a herd of horses in the charge of Flor and Laurentius. The clear colors, the purity, and realistic details are characteristic of the Novgorod school.

7 *Portrait of Pavel Nikolaievich Demidov*, 1773. D. G. Levitsky (1735 to 1822). Oil on canvas, 222.6×166 cm. On the left an inscription on the bench reads: "painted in 1773 by D. Levitsky." Acquired from School of Commerce, St. Petersburg (Leningrad), in the late 1920s. P. N. Demidov (1710–1786) was a mine owner, a keen gardener, and founder of the School of Commerce and the Moscow School of Science Education. In this portrait Demidov is depicted in morning dress with a triumphal colonnade in the background. In the distance we can see the façade of the school. Demidov is resting his left arm on a watering can and points with his right hand to a plant pot, symbols of his enthusiasm for growing exotic plants and of his care for the education of the younger generation.

8 *Portrait of Maria Alexeyevna Dyakova*, 1778. D. G. Levitsky. Oil on canvas, 61×50 cm. Signed on the right on the background: "D. Levitsky. 1778." M. A. Dyakova, Lvova by marriage (1755 to 1807), was the wife of the Russian architect, musician, and art lover, N. A. Lvov. Many poets of the latter half of the 18th century praise Maria Dyakova's charm. While the painting was being restored, poems by Segyur, dedicated to her in French and Russian, were revealed on the back.

9 *Portrait of an unknown woman in Russian national costume*, 1785. I. P. Argunov (1727–1802). Oil on canvas, 67×53.6 cm.

Signed on the left in the background: "I. Argounoff. 1785."
Moved in 1881 from the collection of A. P. Bakhrushin to the
Moscow Museum of History, where it remained until 1930.
Argunov was a serf of Count P. B. Sheremetiev and never had
formal artistic training. The painting possibly depicts a serf
actress in costume.

10 *Wedding ceremony,* 1777. M. Shibanov (latter half of the 18th
century). Oil on canvas, 199×244 cm. Painter's inscription on
the back: "The painting shows the peasants of the Suzdal
province. The wedding ceremony. Painted in the same
province in the village of Tatarov in 1777, Mikhail Shibanov."
Acquired from N. S. Gavrilov in Moscow in 1917. The painting,
one of the first in Russian art on rural life, depicts the traditional
Russian wedding custom of exchanging rings and small presents. M. Shibanov, a serf of Prince Potyomkin, is generally
known as a portrait painter, but he also painted another work
depicting peasant life, *Peasants at their meal.* Both paintings
illustrate the interest that was aroused by the Enlightenment in
the traditions and customs of village inhabitants.

11 *Portrait of the writer, Alexander Sergeievich Pushkin,* 1827. O. A. Kiprensky (1782–1836). Oil on canvas, 63 ×54 cm. Signed bottom
left: "O. K. 1827." The painting was commissioned by
A. A. Delvig. After the latter's death it was acquired by Pushkin,
and in 1916 it was purchased from his estate by the gallery.
Kiprensky painted the portrait in St. Petersburg, in the house of
D. N. Sheremetiev, a patron of the artist. It is a highly authentic
portrayal of the writer, showing his face deep in thought. At the
request of the writer's friends, the bronze figure, top right, of the
muse with a lyre on a golden background was added by
Kiprensky after he had finished working on the portrait. In
recognition of the artist's achievement, Pushkin wrote him
a letter in the form of a poem.

12 *Temple feast,* 1784. I. M. Tankov (1739–1799). Oil on canvas,
102×138 cm. Signed bottom right: "Ivan Tankov 1784." The
painting's composition is strongly reminiscent of theater decoration, which was the artist's original field of work. The painting
shows a Russian village—a subject still rare for Russian painting
in the latter half of the 18th century.

13 *Self-portrait,* 1848. K. P. Bryullov (1799–1852). Oil on cardboard, 64.1×54 cm. From F. I. Pryanishnikov collection, transferred from the Rumyantsev Museum in 1925. This self-portrait,
painted in the artist's last years, illustrates his inner struggle
during a crisis of creativity; romanticism is mixed with precise
psychological analysis.

14 *Head of a boy,* about 1818. V. A. Tropinin (1776–1857). Oil on
canvas, 40.4×32 cm. From P. M. Tretyakov collection. The
portrait of A. V. Tropinin, the artist's son, is one of the best works
of this famous Moscow portrait painter and a vivid illustration of
the traditions of 18th-century art. V. A. Tropinin was a serf and
not released from serfdom until 1823.

15 *Avenue in Albano near Rome,* 1836. M. I. Lebedev (1811–1837). Oil
on canvas, 38×46.2 cm. Signed bottom in the middle: "Lebedev
1836." From P. M. Tretyakov collection. Lebedev, who died
young, reached a peak in his work in Italy, where he mainly
concentrated on landscapes.

16 *Ploughing: spring.* A. G. Venetsianov (1780–1847). Oil on canvas,
51.2×65.5 cm. From P. M. Tretyakov collection. At the beginning of the 1820s, Venetsianov, who was by then a well-known
St. Petersburg portraitist, moved to the country. Soon after,
paintings by him and his pupils on themes of village life appeared
at exhibitions. Venetsianov is regarded as the father of Russian
genre painting. The theme of this painting, linked with the
traditional subjects of the seasons, is a peasant woman driving
horses as an allegory of the coming spring.

17 *The rider* (portrait of Giovanna Paccina, governess in the service
of Countess Y. P. Samoilova), 1832. K. P. Bryullov. Oil on
canvas, 291×206 cm. Signed bottom left: "C. Bruloff
MDCCCXXXII." The collar on the dog running after the horse
bears the inscription: "Samoylo." From P. M. Tretyakov collection. The artist painted this picture in Italy, where he received
the patronage of Y. P. Samoilova. The portrait focuses on the
beauty of the Italian, G. Paccina, but in contrast to other 18th-
century portraits, this painting shows signs of genre style.

18 *The apotheosis of war,* 1871. V. V. Vereshchagin (1842–1904). Oil
on canvas, 127×197 cm. Signed bottom left: "V. Vereshchagin.
1871." From P. M. Tretyakov collection. The painting was
completed during the artist's second trip to Turkestan in 1869 to
1871, and was the last in the series *Barbarians.* Vereshchagin
combined his direct observations of the war with the Central
Asian landscape, bringing in the legend of the despot of the East,
Tamerlane, who left pyramids of human skulls, ruins, and
deserts in his wake. The frame bears the artist's inscription:
"Dedicated to all great conquerors of the past, present, and
future."

19 *The appearance of Christ to the people* (the appearance of the
Messiah), 1837–1857. A. A. Ivanov (1806–1858). Oil on canvas,
540×750 cm. Gift of Tsar Alexander II to the Rumyantsev
Museum, where it remained until 1925. The painting illustrates
the biblical story of John the Baptist, who, while blessing people
on the bank of the Jordan, catches sight of the approaching
Christ and points to him as the savior of mankind. This gigantic
painting was executed in Rome over a period of about twenty
years. It remained unfinished, however, as Ivanov turned away
from Christianity. The painting, which the artist brought back
with him from Italy, aroused great interest among his contemporaries as an attempt to characterize various types of people—
prophets, slaves, pharisees, and warriors—within the basic
framework of the bible story.

20 *The rooks have come,* 1871. A. K. Savrassov (1830–1897). Oil on
canvas, 62×48.5 cm. Signed bottom left: "1871. 'S.' Molvitino.
A. Savrassov." From P. M. Tretyakov collection. This painting
was shown at the first exhibition of the Society of Traveling Art
Exhibitions in 1871. Savrassov was the founder of a school of
Russian landscape painting that strove to reproduce the
distinctive aspects of nature in Russia.

21 *Portrait of the writer, Fyodor Mikhailovich Dostoyevsky,* 1872.
V. G. Perov (1833–1882). Oil on canvas, 99×80.5 cm. Signed
bottom right: "V. Perov May 1872." From P. M. Tretyakov
collection. Dostoyevsky's portrait was commissioned by
P. M. Tretyakov, who had decided to develop a substantial
gallery of portraits of leading personalities in Russian science,

14

culture, and literature. This work is one of the best portrayals of the writer.

22 *Portrait of the writer, Leo Nikolaievich Tolstoy*, 1873. I. N. Kramskoi (1837–1887). Oil on canvas, 98×79.5 cm. Signed bottom right: "I. Kramskoi 1873. September." From P. M. Tretyakov collection. In the summer of 1873, Kramskoi lived quite near Tolstoy's estate, Yasnaya Polyana. In less than one month, the artist painted two portraits, one for P. M. Tretyakov's gallery and one for the writer. Tolstoy liked the portrait and used the artist as a model for the portrait painter, Mikhailov, in the novel *Anna Karenina*.

23 *Boyarynya Morozova*, 1887. V. I. Surikov (1848–1916). Oil on canvas, 304×587.7 cm. Signed bottom right: "V. Surikov. 1887." From P. M. Tretyakov collection. D. L. Mordovtsev's novel, *The Great Division*, provided the theme for this painting. In the middle of the 17th century, Patriarch Nikon introduced a number of church reforms that led to a division of the Church. Boyarynya F. P. Morozova was among Nikon's most fervent opponents. The painting depicts Morozova being taken to the Kremlin for interrogation by Tsar Alexei Mikhailovich. She remained true to her convictions and died in 1679 in exile. Surikov portrayed this event as a popular drama and showed that social problems were a hidden aspect of the division movement. Together with other historic paintings by Surikov, this work depicts a peak in Russian realistic painting.

24 *The morning of the streltsy execution*, 1881. V. I. Surikov. Oil on canvas, 218×379 cm. Signed bottom right: "V. Surikov. 1881." From P. M. Tretyakov collection. The painter portrays the execution of the *streltsy* on Red Square after the last *streltsy* uprising in 1698. The artist tried to express the impact between the old and the new, the reforms of Peter I and the elementary power of the people. The conflict expressed in the looks exchanged between Peter I on horseback and the bearded *streltsy* with the cap focuses the theme sharply.

25 *Water container*, 1902. V. E. Borisov-Musatov (1870–1905). Distemper on canvas, 177×216 cm. Signed bottom left: "V. Musatov. 1902 and 'M' in a circle." Acquired in 1917 from the collection of V. O. Girshman, Moscow. Borisov-Musatov tried to give new life to the refined poetry of upper-class culture. He sympathized with the "Nabis" group of French artists and developed his own Russian version of this art. Typical of his paintings are mat, delicate colors.

26 *Demon*, 1890. M. A. Vrubel (1856–1910). Oil on canvas, 114×211 cm. Acquired in 1908. The main theme of Vrubel's work in the 1890s in painting, printing, and sculpture was the figure of the demon. This figure, which originated in Lermontov's poetry, was to a great extent linked with the conception of symbolism in Russia. The analytic language of form and the coloring are reminiscent of Byzantine mosaic art.

27 *Ivan the Terrible and his son, Ivan, on November 16, 1581*, 1885. I. Y. Repin (1844–1930). Oil on canvas, 199.5×254 cm. Signed bottom right: "I. Repin 1885." From P. M. Tretyakov collection. In this scene Tsar Ivan Vassilyevich Grozny has killed his eldest son in a bout of anger (the writer, V. M. Garshin, posed as the model). The attempt was made with this painting to recreate the atmosphere of a concrete historical event—a common feature in the art of the time.

28 *Portrait of the writer, Leo Nikolaievich Tolstoy*, 1887. I. Y. Repin. Oil on canvas, 124×88 cm. Signed bottom left: "I. Repin 1887, 13–15 August. Yasnaya Polyana." From P. M. Tretyakov collection. The artist came to Yasnaya Polyana to paint the portrait of the writer, who by this time was already famous. In contrast to Kramskoi, who, in the portrait he painted, tried to capture the intellectual in Tolstoy, Repin strove to give a legendary interpretation of the religious philosopher.

29 *Vision of the young Bartholomew*, 1889–90. M. V. Nesterov (1862 to 1942). Oil on canvas, 160×211 cm. Signed bottom left: "Mikhail Nesterov. Ufa." Presented to the gallery by the artist. This painting is one of a series of works on the life of Sergei of Radonezh, founder of the Trinity Monastery of St. Sergius, who was canonized after his death. The scene portrays the encounter between the young Sergei, known as Bartholomew, and the holy old man, who blesses him on his chosen path. The landscape was painted in Abramtsevo, a village near Moscow that was the property of S. I. Mamontov, a well-known patron.

30 *Birch grove*, 1879. A. I. Kuindzhy (1842–1910). Oil on canvas, 97×181 cm. Signed bottom right: "A. Kuindzhy. 1879." From P. M. Tretyakov collection. Kuindzhy, a self-taught artist, possessed amazing skills at experimentation. He worked at the synthesis of space and light and developed a style that considerably influenced the beginning of modern painting in Russia.

31 *Golgotha*, 1892. N. N. Ghe (1831–1894). Oil on canvas, 222.4×191.8 cm. Gift from N. N. Ghe's son in 1897. The painting is an unfinished version of the crucifixion theme. Ghe, a representative of late Romanticism in Russia, tackled questions of Christian morality. Tolstoy and his sermon on "Renouncing violence" greatly influenced the artist. The painting depicts Christ, just before his execution, despairing at the thoughtless cruelty prevalent in the world. *Golgotha*, with its symbolic and expressive features, ushers in the art of the 20th century.

32 *Portrait of N. I. Petrunkevich*, 1893. N. N. Ghe. Oil on canvas, 161.8×114.6 cm. Signed on the left: "1893. N. Ghe." Acquired from N. I. Petrunkevich in 1910. The portrait of N. I. Petrunkevich, Koniskaya by marriage, is one of Ghe's last works. Turning to a traditional subject of 19th-century painting—the portrayal of a woman at an open window—the artist used light distribution to characterize her psychologically.

33 *Eternal peace*, 1894. I. I. Levitan (1861–1900). Oil on canvas, 130×206 cm. Signed bottom left: "I. Levitan. 94." From P. M. Tretyakov collection. This work was painted at Udomlya Lake near Vyshnaya Volotchka. The mournful interpretation of the landscape evokes the old theme of man's ephemeral nature *(vanitas)*. Levitan was a founder of modern landscape painting in Russia.

34 *Windy day: bull*, about 1908. N. P. Krymov (1884–1958). Oil on canvas. This work is one of the first attempts at Expressionist landscape painting in Russia. Its outstanding feature is its naivety.

35 *Man with spectacles* (portrait of K. A. Sünnerberg), 1905–06. M. V. Dobushinski (1875–1957). Paper pasted on cardboard, charcoal, water color, 63×99.6 cm. Signed bottom left in pencil: "M. Dobushinski 1905–06." Acquired in 1908. K. A. Sünnerberg was an art critic, poet, and writer, who wrote under the

pseudonym, K. Erberg. The artist used graphic techniques in an Expressionist style. The subject stands in the center of the composition; behind him is the skyline of St. Petersburg suburbs, anonymous enough to be any large industrial town.

36 *The rape of Europa* (sketch), 1910. V. A. Serov (1865–1911). Distemper on canvas, 71×98 cm. Acquired in 1911. One of Serov's later works, this was created when the artist was filled with impressions from his trip to Greece (1907).

37 *Wisteria*, 1910. M. S. Saryan (1880–1972). Distemper on cardboard, 63×65 cm. Signed bottom left: "M. Saryan 1910." By using extremely vivid colors, the artist strove to reproduce his experience of the passionate nature of the East. This painting is one of the works in his Oriental cycle, which was based on impressions gained during trips to Turkey, Persia, and Egypt.

38 *Red horse bathing*, 1912. K. S. Petrov-Vodkin (1887–1939). Oil on canvas, 160×186 cm. Signed bottom left: "KPV 1912." This painting was exhibited by the artist in 1914; after the exhibition it remained in Sweden; arriving back in the USSR in the 1950s, it was presented to the gallery as a gift. Petrov-Vodkin studied ancient Russian art, Italian early Renaissance, and decorative-heroic interpretation as in Hodler, while developing his style. He worked out a system of space for the structure of his painting which he called "Euclidean," and he applied a spherical perspective.

39 *Portrait of I. A. Morozov*, 1910. V. A. Serov. Oil on canvas, 63.5×77 cm. Signed bottom right: "V. S. 1910." Acquired in 1923 from the Museum of Modern Western European Art. I. A. Morozov (1871–1921), a descendant of the Moscow merchant family Morozov, was a well-known collector of modern French painting. *Fruit and Bronze* by Matisse hangs in the background of the portrait.

40 *Self-portrait with yellow lilies*, 1907. N. S. Goncharova (1881 to 1962). Goncharova's study of Russian icons and her association with Fauvism made her a leading Primitive painter, who oriented her work around Russian popular picture sheets and folk art.

41 *Above the town*, 1914. Marc Chagall (born 1887). Oil on canvas, 141×198 cm. The painting is from the artist's "Vitebsk" period. It was painted in honor of Chagall's engagement to his first wife.

42 *Bleaching linen*, 1917. S. E. Serebryakova (1885–1967). Oil on canvas, 141.8×173.6 cm. Serebryakova is known chiefly for her magnificent portraits and landscapes, but she also uses themes from peasant life. Here she used impressions gained during a stay on her father's estate near Kharkov. A characteristic of her style is a tendency toward the epic and monumental in the portrayal of her subjects.

43 *Petrograd Madonna* (the year 1918 in Petrograd), 1920. K. S. Petrov-Vodkin. Oil on canvas, 72×92 cm. The humanist aspect of revolutionary upheaval is reflected in the poetic form of this working-class woman of Petrograd. The woman's bearing and the colors of her clothes are reminiscent of Russian icons. The scenery of the city in the background suggests Italian Renaissance painting. Certain details (broken windows, a bread line) are concrete indications of the period portrayed in the painting.

44 *Bust of Leo Nikolaievich Tolstoy*, 1899. P. P. Trubetskoi (1867 to 1938). Bronze, 34×33 cm. Acquired in 1911. Trubetskoi is famous as an Impressionist sculptor. He was born in Italy, spent a number of years in various countries, including a few years in Russia, where he made portraits of several Russian intellectuals. Trubetskoi did his studies of Tolstoy, both in sculpture and painting, on the writer's estate in Yasnaya Polyana. Bronze copies of this sculpture are still kept in a number of European cities.

45 *Bust of Alexei Nikolaievich Tolstoy*, 1911. A. S. Golubkina (1864 to 1927). Wood, 66×61 cm. Signed: "A. G." As a pupil of Trubetskoi and Rodin, Golubkina pursued the principles of Impressionism in her sculpture. The wood carver, Ivan Bednyakov, reproduced the plaster model in wood.

46 *Dream*, 1913. S. T. Konenkov (1874–1971). Marble, 36×112 ×53 cm. Signed on left hand and head: "Konenkov." The traditions of Neoprimitivism and Neoclassicism were features of Konenkov's prerevolutionary work. Around 1910 the sculptor created a number of female torsos lying on unworked marble.

47 *Vladimir Ilyich Lenin in the Smolny Institute*, 1930. I. I. Brodski (1884–1939). Oil on canvas, 190×287 cm. Signed bottom left: "I. Brodski." Brodski painted many works with Lenin as the subject. The basis for this painting was a sketch made in 1920 at the opening of the second Congress of the Comintern. The furnishings in Lenin's study are reproduced in detail, as is the figure of Lenin, sitting in an armchair. A copy of this painting is also kept in the Central Lenin Museum in Moscow.

48 *Red furniture*, 1920. R. R. Falk (1886–1958). Oil on canvas, 105.6 ×122.8 cm. Signed bottom left: "1920 F." Falk was an active member of the "Knave of Diamonds" group. He pursued the methods of Cézanne in Russian art and made intensive use of the decorative colorfulness of light.

49 *Future pilots*, 1938. A. A. Deineka (1899–1968). Oil on canvas, 131 ×161 cm. Deineka was one of the founders of the Society of Easel Painting. He strove to achieve an expressive-graphic style. At a time of increasing air travel, he depicts boys who dream of becoming captains of airplanes.

50 *Interrogation of the communists*, 1933. B. V. Yoganzon (1893–1973). Oil on canvas, 211×279 cm. In the thirties the category of great social-history painting emerged in Soviet art. Yoganzon made his name in this field. He followed the traditions of 19th-century Russian realists and in this painting tried to portray a dramatic scene based on the confrontation of greatly contrasting figures: two communists, brought for interrogation before a group of officers of the White Guard who are seated at a table.

51 *A daughter of Soviet Kirghizia*, 1948. S. A. Chuikov (born 1902). Oil on canvas, 120×95 cm. Signed bottom left: "S. Chuikov 48." The artist, who worked often and productively in the Soviet republics of Central Asia, tries to place an expression of new, spiritual self-confidence in people's faces.

52 *Self-portrait in a yellow shirt*, 1943. P. P. Konchalovski (1876 to 1956). Oil on canvas, 122×103 cm. Signed bottom right: "P. Konchalovski 1943." This self-portrait was done in the war years. Konchalovski, who normally tends to depict life in a purely emotional fashion, pursues a different aim here: he portrays himself as a strong-minded artist living imperturbably through those hard times.

16

THE PUSHKIN FINE ARTS MUSEUM

The laying of the foundation stone for the present building of the Pushkin Fine Arts Museum (on Kolomenski Court in Volkhonka Street near the Kremlin and the Moskva River) took place on August 17, 1898. The roots of the museum reach back into the eighteenth century, during which a sizable collection of coins had been assembled at Moscow University. The faculty wanted to put the collection on public display, but they soon found they had to fight for the right to set up even a small gallery.

Developing the museum proved to be a lengthy business, and the collection grew slowly. In 1850, Professor P. M. Leontyev received a few copies of antique sculptures from the Academy of Arts in St. Petersburg for the "collection of fine arts at Moscow University." Another important step was the creation of a chair in the history of art at the university. This led to repeated demands for a museum in Moscow that would provide students with illustrative material for the history of art.

The following generation of university lecturers, especially I. V. Tsvetayev, further pursued the aims of their predecessors. Tsvetayev felt that the museum should serve the public at large as well as students. The idea of democratizing art had spread widely in Russia by the end of the nineteenth century, and a number of museums and galleries of this period opened their doors to broader sections of the population.

Transforming the modest university collection into a modern museum was a tremendous undertaking, hindered by the tsarist government's failure to provide any funds for construction or for the purchase of art works. The founders had to rely on private initiative and especially on the donations of rich patrons like I. S. Nechayev-Maltsev and V. P. Botkin. The complex task included organizing the new institution, constructing a home for it, and simultaneously assembling various collections to fulfill the museum's goals.

Construction of a museum building had already been carried out successfully in Western Europe, but was a new and unusual venture in Russia. Entries were invited in a competition for the best design, and R. I. Klein, who had already designed some Moscow buildings, emerged the winner. Klein's design had a neoclassical façade of marble from the Urals. The building itself was equipped with technical innovations like ceiling lights, central heating, and modern ventilation. The individual halls were decorated in the style of the art works to be displayed. Thus the walls were adorned with copies of classical and Italian frescoes, Byzantine mosaics, and murals, all specially designed for the museum.

On May 31, 1912, the Museum of Fine Arts was officially opened. From the main staircase leading to the second floor, visitors can read a Greek inscription, which means: "What is best in the world is the appreciation of beauty."

Most of the early exhibits were sculptures. Tsvetayev commissioned famous sculptors to produce copies of Russian and Western European works from various epochs. The standard for these copies was high. Some of the artisans came to Moscow to finish their work on the spot. The copies of Cretan-Mycenaean, Greek, and Roman works of art, supplemented by a collection of exquisite vases, which are originals, enabled visitors to experience the art of ancient times. In addition, there was a wealth of medieval and Renaissance sculptures.

The basis for the painting collection was provided in 1909 by a donation from the collector, M. S. Shchekin. This included paintings by German

17

and Italian masters of the thirteenth to seventeenth centuries.

The Egyptian section is based on the collection of the Russian orientalist, V. S. Golenishchev. Acquired by the museum in 1909, it consists almost exclusively of originals and comprises sculptures, artifacts, inscriptions, Faiyum portraits, and Coptic materials. The collection was placed in two halls, where it is still exhibited today. One of the halls was built in the style of an Ancient Egyptian temple.

The nationalization of art collections after the 1917 Revolution and the accompanying redistribution of museum treasures on scientific lines led to a reorganization of the museum under the director, N. I. Romanov. In 1921, the decision was made to open a picture gallery. In 1923, authority over the museum was transferred from the university to the People's Commissariat for Education.

When the Rumyantsev Museum was closed in 1924, its inventory was divided between the Tretyakov Gallery and the Museum of Fine Arts. The items transferred to the museum included a good selection of prints by old masters such as Dürer, Rembrandt, and Callot, which helped considerably to fulfill the print section's goal of covering the history of prints as completely as possible. Art of the twentieth century is represented through, for example, prints by Brenquin, Kollwitz, and Favorski. A collection of popular Russian prints was added from D. P. Rovinsky's legacy, as were Japanese woodcuts (about thirty thousand), drawings (about ten thousand), and a vast collection of bookmarks and bookplates.

On November 10, 1924, the Museum of Fine Arts, enlarged by new collections, was reopened to the public. The gallery of Western European painting consisted of two halls containing works by Dutch and German masters. A year later, at the beginning of September, 1925, three new halls were added, in which Italian paintings of the thirteenth to seventeenth centuries, French paintings of the twelfth to nineteenth centuries, and works of the Barbizon school were exhibited. In 1927, the last hall was opened, containing paintings by Spanish and Flemish masters of the seventeenth century.

In the first few years of Soviet rule, the gallery of Western European painting was enlarged and considerably changed. In 1924 several hundred paintings were sent from Leningrad to Moscow, now the capital. In the same year the Museum of Fine Arts received works by van Goyen, Heda, Ruysdael, Terborch, Lancret, Boucher, and Fragonard, which came from the former Shchukin and Ostroukhov collections and from castles and country residences belonging to the aristocratic families Yusupov and Shuvalo.

Even though the collection was now an important one, containing some very valuable individual items, it still lacked the kinds of works that would give it world renown. For this reason, at the instigation of the well-known art historian, V. N. Lazarev, masterpieces by Rembrandt, Poussin, Titian, Rubens, and van Dyck were transferred in 1925, 1927, and 1928 from the Hermitage in Leningrad to the Museum of Fine Arts in Moscow.

In 1937, on the hundredth anniversary of his death, the museum was named after the great writer, Pushkin. Since then its full name has been the A. S. Pushkin State Museum of Fine Arts.

In 1948, the scope of the museum's collection of Western European painting still did not go beyond the middle of the nineteenth century. But after the museum received a number of late nineteenth- and twentieth-century works from the State Museum for Modern Western European Art, it finally ranked among the best in the world.

A word on the Museum for Modern Western European Art is in order here because of its effect on the Pushkin Museum of Fine Arts. Founded in 1923, it consisted of the nationalized property of the modern art collectors, S. I. Shchukin and I. A. Morozov. Shchukin's collection comprised over two hundred paintings, mainly by French Impressionists, Postimpressionists, Fauvists, and Cubists. The earliest acquired work is the Swiss landscape, *Mountain hut* by Courbet. The first painting for the collection of modern French masters was the *Argenteuil lilac* by Monet, acquired in 1897. Picasso is well represented with fifty paintings—more than any other artist in the museum. Shchukin owned about forty paintings by Matisse, including such famous works as *The dance* and *The music,* which he had commissioned. He had also requested Matisse to come to Moscow in 1911, so that his paintings could be hung under the artist's personal direction.

In his work as a Moscow collector, I. A. Morozov followed his younger brother, M. A. Morozov, who died in 1903. The first painting that I. A. Morozov

18

acquired was *Frost in Louveciennes* by Sisley. Whereas Shchukin bought experimental art by modern painters, Morozov was more attracted by the artists from the "Nabis" group, for instance, Bonnard, Vuillard, and Denis.

In Paris, in the early 1900s, Shchukin and I. A. Morozov were in contact with Durand-Ruel, Druet, A. Vollard, and D.-H. Kahnweiler. Through their acquisitions, interest in French art, which had begun as far back as the eighteenth century, grew enormously. It is possible that French art dealers kept their prices down for Russian customers in order to corner a new market in art for themselves. But Shchukin and Morozov did not rely solely on dealers. They sought advice from such famous Russian painters as Serov and K. A. Korovin and often concluded contracts directly with French painters, for example, Matisse and Denis.

The works from the Museum for Modern Western European Art rounded out the Pushkin Museum collection, creating a representative survey of the main stages in the development of Western European painting.

During the Second World War the museum's treasures were evacuated from Moscow. At the beginning of October, 1946, however, the halls were reopened to visitors. There was even an exhibition of masterpieces from the Dresden Art Gallery, which the Red Army had rescued in the closing days of the war in Europe. As a result of the desire of the Soviet government to strengthen and improve friendly relations between the Soviet and German people, these works were returned to the German Democratic Republic in 1955.

After 1955, the permanent exhibitions of copies of statues and paintings in the halls of the Pushkin Museum were redesigned, with special attention paid to the section on paintings. It currently numbers over two thousand works from various epochs and schools.

Among its most treasured exhibits is the museum's collection of original French painting. The seventeenth century is represented by excellent works by Lebrun, Poussin *(The noble courage of Scipio, The holy family, Rinaldo and Armida, Heroic landscape with Hercules)*, Vuiller, Valentin, and Lorrain *(Landscape with a bridge, The rape of Europa)*. They are a reflection of the period's classicism and the style of Caravaggio in France.

Royal portraits of the eighteenth century can be found in the work of Mignard, Largillière, Rigaud, Toquet, and Duplessis. Portraits by Drouais, Voile, and Nattier are also worthy of note. A wide selection of paintings by C. Vernet, Hubert Robert, Fragonard, Watteau, Lancret, Boucher, and Greuze illustrates the character of their times with great skill and unusual expressiveness. The still lifes by Chardin and Oudry as well as the *Charlatan* by Debucourt and Boily's *Workshop* are all delightful.

Early nineteenth-century works on display are by J.-L. David, Guérin, Gros, M. Gérard, C. Vernet, Géricault, and Delacroix. An important section of nineteenth-century art includes paintings of the Barbizon school collected by S. M. Tretyakov and P. I. Kharitonenko. The works of Dupret, Rousseau, Daubigny, Diaz de la Peña, and Troyon clearly depict the various painting styles employed by this school. The most notable mid nineteenth-century French artists are Corot (14 paintings, including *Diana bathing* and *The gust of wind)*, Millet, Bastien-Lepage, Meissonier, Breton, Laermaus, Dechamps, and Courbet. Impressionism is well represented, with examples of Monet's several creative stages and with works by Renoir, Degas, Sisley, and Pissarro. The new movement in art, evolving from Impressionism, is depicted in the gallery by the works of Cézanne, van Gogh, Gauguin, Signac, Toulouse-Lautrec, and the painters in the "Nabis" group. For these artists the impression made on the viewer was far more important than a realistic reproduction of the subject. The artistic experiments of the Fauvists portrayed a new spirit, as can be seen in the numerous works by Matisse, Derain, and Vlaminck. Cubist painting is represented by Picasso. And, to round off the section on French art, we have sculptures by Rodin, Maillol, and Bourdelle.

The gallery of Western European painting also has a large selection of seventeenth-century Dutch painting, including a substantial number of paintings by Rembrandt and his successors (Lievens, de Gelder, Bol, Paudiss, N. Knüpfer). The once widely available genre paintings are represented in works by Metsu, Steen, Ostade, Peter de Hooch, and Terborch. There are also portraits by van der Helst, Netscher, and W. van der Vliet and landscapes by van Goyen, Cuyp, van der Velde, Ruysdael, van der Neer, Weenix, and Both. There is a good collection of still lifes by Heda, de Heem, Kalf, and other painters. The

19

seventeenth-century Flemish school covers primarily paintings and sketches by Rubens and Jordaens and still lifes by Snyders.

A notable feature of the section on Italian Renaissance art is the polyptych by Botticelli. There is a considerable number of Byzantine icons and early Italian works that were greatly influenced by the Byzantine style of painting (thirteenth century). Sixteenth-century portrait painting can be found in works by Bronzino, Parmigianino, and del Piombo. Some mention should also be made of the works of the seventeenth-century Italians, Guercino, Dolci, Magnasco, and Crespi. Individual paintings by, for example, Strozzi, Guardi, Canaletto, and Pannini represent the eighteenth-century Italian masters.

The sections on old German and Dutch art are not strong but nevertheless portray the characteristics of the national schools. Nineteenth-century German art can be seen in a few paintings by Menzel, Knaus, and Wothe.

The Pushkin Museum's collections are continually expanding. The works of modern artists are being added, often in the form of gifts (for example, paintings of the American artist, Rockwell Kent). In the 1920s purchases were made of paintings by Miró, Chirico, and Léger. There are frequent large special exhibitions of items from leading collections throughout Europe and the United States, including an exhibition of paintings by progressive artists from the west like Renato Guttuso and Giacomo Manzú.

Experts in the museum's workshops see to the preservation and restoration of the art works. New acquisitions are registered iconographically, and the data are placed in the archives. One of the museum's chief fields of work is researching the southern part of the USSR. Archeological excavations in the towns of Kherzonez, Feodossia, and Tanaiz have uncovered classical treasures from the periods of Greek and Roman colonization. A great deal of interest has been generated by these finds, which are on display in the sections on classical art.

NOTES ON ILLUSTRATIONS

53 *Portrait of a boy with a golden wreath*, early 2nd century A. D. Unknown Faiyum master. Wood, encaustic, 21×35.5 cm. From V. S. Golenishchev's collection in 1911. This portrait is included in the museum's unique Faiyum portrait collection. The style reflects the transition from an illusionistic conception to greater idealization and spiritualization in Roman art. Faiyum portraits were named after the oasis, Faiyum, near Cairo, where they were first found in the late 1880s. They are painted on wood panels that were used to cover the faces of the deceased, thus replacing the sculptured masks of the Ancient Egyptian burial rites.

54 *The 12 Apostles*, first half of the 14th century. Unknown Byzantine master. Distemper on wood, 38×34 cm. Acquired in 1932 from the Museum of History in Moscow. This icon originated in a Constantinople workshop in the "Palaeologus Renaissance"— the last period in the development of Byzantine art. The colors are light green, dark green, olive green, and lilac-gray, which were typical of that time.

55 *Saint Sebastian*, Giovanni Antonio Boltraffio (1467–1516). Oil on canvas, 48×36 cm, transferred from wood to canvas in 1860. Acquired in 1930 from the Hermitage. This painting was probably created toward the end of the 15th century when Boltraffio was working in Leonardo da Vinci's studio in Milan. Scientists believe that the facial features of St. Sebastian bear a resemblance to Salai, a pupil of Leonardo.

56 *Mary enthroned with the Christ child*, about 1280. Unknown Italian master. Distemper on wood, 173×84 cm. Acquired in 1925 from the Museum of Smolensk. This icon was painted by artists of the Pisa school. In that period Pisa had cultural and trade links with Byzantium, and numerous Byzantine craftsmen worked in Pisa. The icon shows traces of Byzantine and late Romanesque styles.

57, *St. Laurentius* and *St. Stephen*. Stefano di Giovanni (known as
58 Il Sassetta, 1392–1450). Distemper on wood, each part 76×25 cm. *St. Laurentius* and *St. Stephen* form altar wings. Late Gothic features can clearly be seen in this work, painted by one of the most important artists of the 15th-century Siena school.

59 *The Annunciation*. Alessandro di Mariano Filipepi (known as Botticelli, 1445–1510). Distemper on canvas, each part 45×13 cm. Acquired in 1928 from the Hermitage. This work consists of two parts: *Madonna Annunziata* and *The Archangel Gabriel*. It is believed that these two wings, together with the others from the Hermitage, were once part of the predella of a large altar composition, painted in the 1490s. *The Annunciation* is a characteristic subject for Florentine artists and is striking in its expressiveness.

60 *Mary with the Christ child*. Lucas Cranach the Elder (1472–1553). Oil on wood, 58×46 cm. The painting is cut deeply around the edges. Acquired in 1930 from the Hermitage. This work was painted quite late in the artist's life. It was possibly part of a large altar.

61 *The holy family*. Agnolo Tori Bronzino (1503–1572). Oil on canvas, 117×99 cm (transferred from wood to canvas in 1857). Acquired in 1932 from the State Antique Market in Leningrad. 20

This Mannerist painter was famous for his portraits. Here the theme is religious: Mary with the infant, John the Baptist, and Joseph. It was probably painted between 1555 and 1560.

62 *Landscape with scenes from the lives of saints.* Dosso Dossi (real name: Giovanni Luteri, 1479–1542). Oil on canvas, 60×87 cm. Acquired in 1933 from the History of Religion Museum in Moscow. This painting was identified by V. N. Lazarev. Saints are portrayed at various points of the landscape: St. Francis inflicting stigmata on himself, St. Jerome with the cross, St. Catherine, St. Christopher with young Jesus on his shoulder, and St. George fighting the dragon. The landscape, however, with its intense green colors, dominates the painting.

63 *Minerva.* Paolo Caliari (known as Veronese, 1528–1588). Oil on canvas, 28×16 cm. Acquired from the Hermitage. The pendant to *Minerva*—the sketch of *Diana*—can be seen in the Hermitage. Both works were executed in a free manner, characteristic of Venetian painters, who were attempting to reintroduce the cheerful world of the High Renaissance as opposed to the serious, religious concept of Mannerism. *Minerva* was obviously a study intended to decorate a country villa.

64 *Coquettish old woman,* 1630. Bernardo Strozzi (1581–1644). Oil on canvas, 136×110 cm. Acquired in 1924 from the Rumyantsev Museum. B. R. Wipper identified the painting; earlier it was attributed to Johann Leis. The figure of the servant girl can be found in other paintings by Strozzi. The Genoese painter linked Caravaggio's style with elements of the Flemish school. This painting is from the Venetian period of his work. The scene is an allegory of the transience of life.

65 *Apotheosis of Duchess Isabella,* 1635. Peter Paul Rubens (1577 to 1640). Oil on wood, 68×75 cm. Acquired in 1930 from the Hermitage. Study of the triumphal arch in honor of the coming to Antwerp of the Governor of the Netherlands, the cardinal, and the infant Ferdinand.

66 *Bacchanalia,* about 1615. Peter Paul Rubens. Oil on canvas, 91×107 cm. Acquired in 1930 from the Hermitage. This painting, which is full of sensuous power, presents an allegory of the harvest festival in Autumn, personified by figures of fertility.

67 *Still life with a swan.* Frans Snyders (1579–1657). Oil on canvas, 162×228 cm. Signed bottom left: "F. Sny." (The last few letters of the artist's name are missing, as they were on the part of the canvas that was attached to the easel and lost when the painting was shortened and trimmed.) Acquired in 1930 from the Hermitage. This work was painted in the 1620s and combines the styles found in the still lifes *Hunting Trophies* and *Gifts of Nature.*

68 *Satyr visiting a peasant,* about 1621. Jacob Jordaens (1593–1678). Oil on canvas, 153×205 cm. Acquired in 1930 from the Hermitage. This work was painted in an early period of creativity of the Flemish artist. It depicts an Aesop fable, which tells of a satyr's encounter with a peasant, who blew into his hands to warm them up and into hot soup to cool it down. Jordaens, fascinated by this ancient subject, saw it as an example of the duality of human behavior and transposed the fable to his own time. It was also used on several occasions by baroque painters.

69 *David with Goliath's head.* Domenico Fetti (1588/89–1624). Oil on canvas, 107×82 cm. Acquired in 1930 from the Hermitage. Fetti, like Strozzi, was influenced by Caravaggio, Rubens, and Veronese. His paintings on biblical themes have genre character. He painted *David with Goliath's head* when he was in the service of the Duke of Mantua.

70 *Ahasver, Haman, and Esther,* 1660. Rembrandt Harmensz van Rijn (1606–1669). Oil on canvas, 73×94 cm. Signed bottom left: "Rembrandt: F. 1660." Acquired in 1924 from the Rumyantsev Museum; prior to 1882 in the Hermitage. This painting was originally attributed to the Rembrandt school. Its true origin was identified in 1899 by Dr. Bredius, the director of the Royal Art Gallery in The Hague. It was restored in the early 1970s, and is considered one of the artist's major works. It is based on the biblical legend of the Jewess, Esther, wife of the Persian king, Ahasver. When Haman, the king's confidant, persuaded Ahasver to destroy the Jewish people, Esther found out and resolved to intercede for her people. She invited Haman to a feast with her and the king and denounced him in front of Ahasver. The painting depicts the scene where Esther has just come to the end of her tale.

71 *Portrait of an old woman,* 1654. Rembrandt Harmensz van Rijn. Oil on canvas, 82×72 cm. Signed bottom right: "Rembrandt F. 1654." Acquired in 1929 from the Hermitage. This painting is from Rembrandt's second period of creativity which started about 1632 and lasted around ten years. The artist lived in Amsterdam at that time and was in very great demand as a portrait painter. His artistic development is characterized by softened effects of light and shade and a greater use of color.

72 *The peasants' wedding.* Jan Steen (1626–1679). Oil on wood, 35×44 cm. Signed bottom right: "J. S." Acquired in 1928 from the Hermitage. Steen painted scenes from the life of the aristocracy and from the everyday lives of the petty bourgeoisie and peasants. This genre painting shows the love of detail characteristic of the Dutch.

73 *The sick child.* Pieter de Hooch (1629 to about 1683). Oil on canvas, 52×61 cm. Signed on the left: "P. Hoogh." Acquired in 1927 from the Hermitage. As in most of his paintings, de Hooch displays here an interest in the everyday life of the middle classes. He often depicted women and children in drawing rooms. This painting, which evidently dates back to the 1650s as de Hooch later turned to portraying wealthier families, is noted for its muted coloring, clearly defined, enclosed spaces, and balanced harmony of light and shade.

74 *The peasants' feast.* Adriaen van Ostade (1610–1685). Oil on canvas, 102×137 cm. Signed bottom right: "A. Ostade." Acquired in 1927 from the Hermitage. This work, incorporating elements from Hals and Brouwer, was painted when the artist was at his peak.

75 *Heroic landscape with Hercules,* probably 1665. Nicolas Poussin (1594–1665). Oil on canvas, 156×202 cm. Acquired in 1927 from the Hermitage. This painting is a pendant to the *Landscape with Polyphemos* in the Hermitage. It was always believed that the work dated from 1649, but recent research shows it to have been painted in 1665. Its theme is taken from the eighth book of the *Aeneid,* of the Roman poet Virgil, depicting the fight between Hercules and the giant, Cacus. Cacus had stolen the herd of

cattle which Hercules had captured from Geryon, and for this, Hercules slew him. According to Aeneas, Virgil's narrator, this heroic deed was carried out on the Aventine Hill, which later became part of Rome. The *Heroic landscape with Hercules* is a masterpiece of landscape painting by this great French classical painter.

76 *Rinaldo and Armida*. Nicolas Poussin. Oil on canvas, 95×133 cm. Acquired in 1930 from the Hermitage. The scene in this painting is from the fourteenth canto of the epic *Jerusalem Delivered* by the Italian poet, Torquato Tasso (1581). The sorceress, Armida, decided to kill Rinaldo. She enticed him to an island where he was lulled to sleep by zephyrs. But after she saw the sleeping Rinaldo, Armida fell in love with him and took him to her garden.

77 *Rape of Europa*, 1655. Claude Gellée (known as Lorrain, 1600 to 1682). Oil on canvas, 100×137 cm. Signed bottom right: "Claudio G. V. Romae 1655." Acquired in 1927 from the Hermitage. This work was painted in 1655 for Pope Alexander VII. It is based on the Greek legend of Europa, the daughter of a Phoenician king, who was carried off by Zeus. The god appeared to her in the shape of a white bull; he swam across the sea, and the continent to which he brought Europa was named after her. The artist chose an historical landscape for the background. This work had great influence on the development of landscape painting in Europe.

78 *Death of Dido*. Giovanni Battista Tiepolo (1696–1770). Oil on canvas, 40×63 cm. Acquired in 1928 from the Hermitage. The theme is taken from the legend of Dido, a Tyrian king's daughter and founder of Carthage. The Roman poet, Virgil, describes in the *Aeneid* how Dido set herself on fire after discovering that her lover, Aeneas, had been unfaithful. The style of Tiepolo, the most famous master of an 18th-century Venetian line of painters, was typical of baroque monumental painting. According to O. I. Lavrova, this work, which was done in the 1750s, is a study for a cycle of frescoes that were supposed to adorn the Valmarano Villa, but were never painted.

79 *Fish*. Giuseppe Recco (1634–1695). Oil on canvas, 91×127 cm. Acquired in 1924 from the Rumyantsev Museum, to which it had been presented by the Committee for the Protection of Art Treasures in 1919. This painting is the work of an artist of the Neapolitan school who combined Caravaggio's style with the vitality of baroque painting. The paint in this still life is thick and the colors bright.

80 *Bivouac (military camp)*, about 1709–10. Jean Antoine Watteau (1684–1721). Oil on canvas, 32×45 cm. Acquired in 1928 from the Hermitage. This painting is one of a series of war scenes painted by Watteau. It came into being when the young artist went home to Valenciennes from Paris for a short period. One can barely recognize the famous painter of elegant scenes when one first looks at this work on military life. The relationship between figures and landscape, the gentle blending of colors, and the entire composition are, however, characteristic of this rococo artist.

81 *The nuns' meal*. Alessandro Magnasco (1667–1749). Oil on canvas, 94×76 cm. Acquired in 1917 from the Rumyantsev

Museum, to which it had been moved from the Vorstädter collection in 1924. Magnasco is regarded as a major Italian baroque painter. Some of his favorite motifs were scenes from monastic life. The artist bestowed features of religious ecstasy on the genre scene, emphasizing it with the aid of dark colors. The monastic cycle is attributed to the artist's second Milan period.

82 *View of a small Venetian courtyard*. Francesco Guardi (1712–1793). Acquired in 1924 from D. I. Shchukin's collection. The *View of a small Venetian courtyard* is a pendant to *View of Venice*, which can also be found in the Pushkin Museum. In anticipation of the open-air painting of the following century, the artist included a wider variety of lighter colors in some of his works to achieve special light effects. In the 1770s Guardi showed a clear preference for painting such intimate Venetian scenes.

83 *Hercules and Omphale*. François Boucher (1703–1770). Oil on canvas, 90×74 cm. Acquired in 1930 from the Hermitage. The subject of the painting is Hercules as the prisoner of the Lydian queen, Omphale. Greek and Roman mythology was used here, as in most other French rococo works, to depict an erotic scene. Strong colors, modeling, and a wealth of details make this work one of the artist's best.

84 *Maypole festival*. Jean-Baptiste Pater (1695–1736). Oil on canvas, 34.5×44.5 cm. Acquired in 1967. *Maypole festival* is a work by Watteau's one and only pupil, Pater, who followed his teacher's style. This elegant painting is dedicated to the Spring festival and designed as a pastoral scene in rococo. The maypole occupies the middle of the foreground as a traditional symbol of Spring and love.

85 *At the stove*. Jean-Honoré Fragonard (1732–1806). Oil on canvas, 25×35 cm. Acquired in 1924 from the Department of Education in Mozhaisk. This study is an early work of the French painter and still displays elements of Rubens' style.

86 *The approach of the thunderstorm*, 1871. Virgilio Narciso Diaz de la Peña (1807–1878). Oil on wood, 21×30 cm. Signed bottom left: "Diaz 71." In P. I. Kharitonenko's collection till 1920, then in the Rumyantsev Museum from which it was acquired in 1924. As a follower of romantic landscape painting, this artist was influenced by the Barbizon school, as is clearly shown in *The approach of the thunderstorm*. The work portrays a marshy area with low trees and dark clouds. A solitary wanderer appears to be running away from the threatening storm. The light effects and free strokes are elements of romantic painting.

87 *After the shipwreck*. Eugène Delacroix (1798–1863). Oil on canvas, 36×57 cm. Signed bottom left: "Eug. Delacroix." From S. M. Tretyakov collection; in the Tretyakov Gallery until 1925. This small work is believed to have been painted toward the end of the 1830s or the beginning of the 1840s. It is probably on the theme of the painting, *Don Juan's Boat*, completed in 1841, which can be seen in the Louvre. The turbulent scene, free strokes, and strong colors mark Delacroix as an important French romantic painter.

88 *Andromache weeping over Hector*, 1783. Jacques-Louis David (1748–1825). Oil on canvas, 58×43 cm. Signed bottom left: "L. David 1783." Acquired in 1927 from the Hermitage. This work is a study for a painting that can be seen in the École des

Beaux-Arts Museum in Paris. The painting, drawn from the *Iliad*, depicts Troy's defender, Hector, who is slain fighting against Achilles. Andromache, Hector's wife, together with her son, Astianakes, weeps over the dead man. Several of David's works, which were painted on the eve of the French Revolution, were aimed at strengthening the courage and fighting spirit of the bourgeoisie. By mobilizing all his artistic forces, David strove to achieve the clear plastic form characteristic of late French classicism.

89 *True love*, 1882. Jules Bastien-Lepage (1848–1884). Oil on canvas, 194×179 cm. Signed at the bottom: "J. Bastien-Lepage. Damvilliers 1882." Acquired in 1925 from the S. M. Tretyakov collection. As a student of the École des Beaux-Arts in Paris, Bastien-Lepage took up Millet's themes but gave them sentimental or religious character. His esthetic position was soon defined through the influence of the rapidly developing neorealistic school in France. This painting is a typical example of Salon painting on rural themes.

90 *Frost in Louveciennes*, 1873. Alfred Sisley (1839–1899). Oil on canvas, 46×61 cm. Signed bottom left: "Sisley 73." Bought from P. Durand-Ruel for I. A. Morozov's collection in 1903 where it remained until 1918; then to the Museum for Modern Western European Art in 1948. This painting was the first French work of art which I. A. Morozov acquired for his collection.

91 *Poor fishermen*, 1879. Pierre Puvis de Chavannes (1824–1898). Oil on canvas, 65×91 cm. Signed on the right: "P. Puvis de Ch. 79." In S. I. Shchukin collection until 1918, then the Museum for Modern Western European Art from which it was acquired in 1948. This study for a painting of the same name, which can be seen in the Louvre in Paris, is an example of the work of a 19th-century reformer of mural painting.

92 *The gust of wind*. Jean-Baptiste Camille Corot (1796–1875). Oil on canvas, 48×66 cm. Signed bottom left: "Corot." Acquired in 1925 from the S. M. Tretyakov collection in the Tretyakov Gallery. This work dates from the late 1860s, when the artist was working on several other paintings with similar titles. The style of the painter changed greatly in this period. Under the influence of the Barbizon school, the artist eventually romanticized landscape motifs. He showed preference for the atmospheric changes between night and day and a soft lyrical treatment of light. In his later works he came close to Impressionism.

93 *Rouen Cathedral at midday*, 1894. Claude Oscar Monet (1840 to 1926). Oil on canvas, 100×65 cm. Signed bottom left: "Claude Monet, 94." Bought from P. Durand-Ruel for the S. I. Shchukin collection where it remained until 1918; then in the Museum for Modern Western European Art from which it was acquired in 1948. This work is one of a series of paintings of Rouen Cathedral done between 1892 and 1895. Two works from this group, painted in 1894, can be found in the Pushkin Museum. Twenty paintings from the series were exhibited at Durand-Ruel's in 1895. Monet is regarded as the father of Impressionism. With the series of cathedral paintings, Monet aimed at capturing the changes that arise from varying light conditions and times of day and different seasons. The entire cycle can be split into the groups, *Morning, Daytime,* and *Evening*. Monet worked on these paintings both at the cathedral and in his studio.

94 *Mountain hut*. Gustave Courbet (1819–1877). Oil on canvas, 33×49 cm. Signed bottom right: "G. Courbet." In S. I. Shchukin collection until 1918; then in the Museum for Modern Western European Art from which it was acquired in 1948. This landscape was painted by the French artist in Switzerland, where he lived in exile after the Paris Commune. His use of mastic in this painting later became characteristic of Courbet's work.

95 *In Luxembourg park*, 1876. Adolph Menzel (1815–1905). Oil on canvas, 21×27 cm. Signed bottom left: "Ad. Menzel, 76." Acquired in 1925 from the S. M. Tretyakov collection in the Tretyakov Gallery. This work by the famous German painter is striking through the directness and clarity of its composition. Artistic solutions of this nature ordinarily could be found only in French painting of that time.

96 *Collecting wood*. Jean-François Millet (1814–1875). Oil on canvas, 37×45 cm. Signed bottom right: "J. F. Millet." Acquired in 1925 from the S. M. Tretyakov collection in the Tretyakov Gallery. Toward the end of the 1840s, Millet moved to the village of Barbizon and devoted his time, under T. Rousseau's influence, to landscape painting. *Collecting wood* was painted in the 1850s. In this work, which is typical of the decade, women are portrayed doing heavy work in a dark and dense forest.

97 *Luncheon on the grass*, 1866. Claude Oscar Monet. Oil on canvas, 130×181 cm. Signed bottom left: "Claude Monet 66." In S. I. Shchukin's collection until 1918; then in the Museum for Modern Western European Art from which it was acquired in 1948. This painting is an attempt at developing further Manet's *Luncheon in the open*, 1863, Paris, Museum of Impressionism. He painted the first version in the village of Chaille, and his models included Camille Dancier (his future wife) and the painters, Frédéric Bazille and Albert Lambron. He finished it in Paris, but was dissatisfied with it and so painted a second, smaller version. This painting, in which Monet increased the number of people, is in darker shades of color than the fragments that have survived from the first version. The contrast between light and shade is also not so marked here.

98 *Portrait of the actress, Jeanne Samary*, 1877. Pierre Auguste Renoir (1841–1919). Oil on canvas, 56×47 cm. Signed top left: "Renoir 77." Bought at P. Durand-Ruel's in 1904 for I. A. Morozov's collection where it remained until 1918; then in the Museum for Modern Western European Art from which it was acquired in 1948. Jeanne Samary (1857–1890) was an actress at the Comédie Française. She made her first appearance as Corinne in *Tartuffe* by Molière. She later played classical soubrettes. Renoir is known to have painted four portraits of Samary. The one in the Pushkin Museum was shown at the third exhibition of the Impressionists. Many art historians regard this portrait as one of the best Renoir ever painted. Jeanne Samary's portrait (1878) is kept in the Hermitage.

99 *In the garden under trees*, 1875. Pierre Auguste Renoir. Oil on canvas, 81×65 cm. Signed bottom right: "Renoir." Bought at

23

G. Villeau's in 1907 for I. A. Morozov's collection where it remained until 1918; then in the Museum for Modern Western European Art from which it was acquired in 1948. The same models were used in this painting as in *Dance at the Moulin de la Galette* (1876, Museum of Impressionism, Paris): Jeanne, the artist, Franc Lamic, Guenette, and the art critic and writer, George Rivier. This work was painted in the garden of a house in Rue Courtauld where Renoir's studio was situated. *The Swing* (Museum of Impressionism, Paris) was also painted in this garden.

100 *Nude,* 1876. Pierre Auguste Renoir. Oil on canvas, 92×73 cm. Signed bottom right: "Renoir 76." Bought at P. Durand-Ruel's for S. I. Shchukin's collection where it remained until 1918; then in the Museum for Modern Western European Art from which it was acquired in 1948. It is generally thought that the model for this painting was the same Anna as in Manet's *Nana*. It was shown at the Impressionists' second exhibition with the title *Study*. A preliminary sketch exists for it in the Museum of Impressionism in Paris.

101 *Dancers in blue,* about 1899. Edgar Degas (1834–1917). Pastel on paper, 64×65 cm. Signed top left: "Degas." Bought at P. Durand-Ruel's for S. I. Shchukin's collection where it stayed until 1918; then in the Museum for Modern Western European Art from which it was acquired in 1948. In his last active years (Degas went blind in 1900), the artist strove toward a synthesis of form, relying more on his own memories than on the study of nature. The *Dancers in blue* is one of his best works, distinguished by its precise handling of the monochrome range of colors and of the decorative rhythm that is reminiscent of *The Dancers*, 1899, in the Cleveland Museum of Art in the United States.

102 *Pierrot and Harlequin,* 1888. Paul Cézanne (1839–1906). Oil on canvas, 102×81 cm. Bought at P. Durand-Ruel's in 1904 for S. I. Shchukin's collection where it stayed until 1918; then in the Museum for Modern Western European Art from which it was acquired in 1948. Another title for this painting is *Carnival Week*. It was either painted in the artist's studio in Rue Valle de Gras in Paris or, according to other sources, in Aix. Pierrot is on the left and Harlequin on the right. The models were the painter, L. Gigoni (Pierrot), and Cézanne's son, Paul (Harlequin). Preliminary studies in oil and five drawings are known to exist for Harlequin.

103 *Peaches and pears.* Paul Cézanne. Oil on canvas, 61×90 cm. Bought in 1912 at A. Vollard's for I. A. Morozov's collection where it remained until 1918; then in the Museum for Modern Western European Art from which it was acquired in 1948. Cézanne is noted in this painting for his renewed consolidation of form, which did not, however, derive from emphasizing the drawing but developed from the coloring. He used this method of composition in still lifes as well as in landscape and portrait painting.

104 *The plain at the mountain of Sainte-Victoire.* Paul Cézanne. Oil on canvas, 58×72 cm. Bought at A. Vollard's in 1907 for I. A. Morozov's collection where it remained until 1918; then in the Museum for Modern Western European Art from which it was acquired in 1948. This landscape was painted in the early 1880s when Cézanne was working in Aix and its surroundings. The painting depicts the valley with the mountain of Sainte-Victoire. The range of colors covers combinations of orange, green, and blue which the artist used to define clearly each area; he thus overcame the diffusive tendencies of many Impressionists.

105 *Red vineyards in Arles,* 1888. Vincent van Gogh (1853–1890). Oil on canvas, 75×93 cm. In I. A. Morozov's collection until 1918; then in the Museum for Modern Western European Art from which it was acquired in 1948. The painting was shown at the "XX" exhibition in Brussels in 1890 and was purchased by the Dutch painter, Anna Bosch. It is one of the two works sold while van Gogh was still alive. It was painted during a visit made by the artist to Arles (February 1888 to May 1889), presumably after Gauguin, who had worked there with him, had left.

106 *Prisoners' exercise,* 1890. Vincent van Gogh. Oil on canvas, 80×64 cm. Acquired in 1948 from the Museum for Modern Western European Art. This painting is an independent copy of the famous engraving by Gustave Doré. It was painted during van Gogh's convalescence in Saint-Rémy hospital (February 1890) when he, on his doctor's recommendation, made copies of engravings by Rembrandt, Millet, Delacroix, Daumier, and Doré.

107 *L'Avenue de l'Opéra in Paris,* 1898. Camille Pissarro (1830–1903). Oil on canvas, 65×82 cm. Signed bottom right: "C. Pissarro, 98." Bought at P. Durand-Ruel's for S. I. Shchukin's collection where it remained until 1918; then in the Museum for Modern Western European Art from which it was acquired in 1948. This work was painted in the winter of 1897–98 from a window of the Hotel du Louvre, and constitutes one of Pissarro's six most famous works on the same theme. This series of views of Paris are late works by the artist when he, together with G. Seurat, P. Signac, and his son, Lucien Pissarro, turned to neo-Impressionism. Pissarro strove toward a synthesis of Impressionist traditions in portraying the modern city. The series was designed to show the continually changing light at different times of day.

108 *The singer, Yvette Gilbert,* 1894. Henri de Toulouse-Lautrec (1864–1901). Distemper on cardboard, 57×42 cm. Signed bottom left: "T. Lautrec 94." In I. A. Morozov collection until 1903; then in the Museum for Modern Western European Art from which it was acquired in 1948. This is a painting of the popular French singer, Yvette Gilbert. Lautrec often made portraits of her (water colors in the Toulouse-Lautrec Museum in Albi). This portrait was painted by the artist at the end of November 1894 for the periodical *Le Rire*.

109 *Café in Arles,* 1888. Paul Gauguin (1848–1903). Oil on canvas, 72×92 cm. Signed twice, on the billiard table and bottom right: "P. Gauguin 88." In I. A. Morozov collection until 1918; then in the Museum for Modern Western European Art from which it was acquired in 1948. This work, which portrays Madame Genou, was painted at the same time as van Gogh's *The Night Café* during their joint stay in Arles. (There is a charcoal sketch of it in a private collection in the United States.) Gauguin wrote a letter to the artist, E. Bernard, describing the painting, although there are differences in the

description from the final version. Presumably the painting was finished a while later, with the addition of two figures in the background. This is also indicated by the two signatures.

110 *Woman's profile in a window*. Odilon Redon (1840–1916). Pastel on cardboard, 63×49 cm. Signed bottom left: "Odilon Redon." In S. I. Shchukin collection until 1918; then in the Museum for Modern Western European Art from which it was acquired in 1948. Redon was a member of the same generation as the Impressionists, but he was not influenced by them and reproached them with lacking in imagination. He created a world of mysterious forces in his works. He was also acquainted with Symbolist writers.

111 *Polyphem*, 1907. Maurice Denis (1870–1943). Oil on canvas, 81×116 cm. Signed bottom left: "Maurice Denis 1907." In I. A. Morozov collection until 1918; then in the Museum for Modern Western European Art from which it was acquired in 1948. Denis, a founding member of the "Nabis" group, developed his theory of symbolism in painting. He chose religious and mythological themes for his paintings and tended toward decorative styles.

112 *The artist's studio*, 1911. Henri Matisse (1863–1954). Oil on canvas, 181×221 cm. Signed bottom right: "Henri Matisse 1911." In S. I. Shchukin collection until 1918; acquired in 1948 from the Museum for Modern Western European Art. This painting depicts a section of Matisse's studio (the section to the left can be seen in the painting *The Red Studio*, 1911, Museum of Modern Art, New York). Well-known works by the artist hang on the walls, a decorative figure in bronze (Baquin collection, New York) stands on a pedestal on the left, the painting, *Luxuriance* (Copenhagen, City Museum, second version, 1907), hangs behind it, and on the right we can see the left-hand side of the mural *Dance* (Museum of Modern Art, New York, 1909 version).

113 *Goldfish*, 1911. Henri Matisse. Oil on canvas, 147×98 cm. Bought from the artist in 1912 for the S. I. Shchukin collection where it remained until 1918; then in the Museum for Modern Western European Art from which it was acquired in 1948. Matisse painted more than ten aquarium works; the most famous of this series is the one in the Pushkin Museum.

114 *Mirror over a commode*, about 1908. Pierre Bonnard (1867–1947). Oil on canvas. Signed bottom right: "Bonnard." In I. A. Morozov collection until 1918; then in the Museum for Modern Western European Art from which it was acquired in 1948. Bonnard was a founding member of the "Nabis" group. His major works consist of genre paintings, landscapes, and nudes with subtle gradation of color. The *Nue* series is particularly well-known. The Moscow work was painted in the same year as the *Nude against the light* in the Museum of Fine Arts in Brussels. It is believed that the model for both paintings was Marthe Boursin.

115 *Landscape in Auvers*, 1925. Maurice Vlaminck (1876–1958). Oil on canvas, 45×55 cm. Signed: "Vlaminck." Bought in Paris in 1925 for the Museum for Modern Western European Art from which it was acquired in 1948. Vlaminck retired to Auvers in the 1920s and painted a large number of landscapes of this region. The period is characterized by the predominance of blue

enlivened by white and red. These poetic works of nature seem like a lyrical diary of the artist's life.

116 *Pont Saint-Michel in Paris*, 1908. Pierre Albert Marquet (1875 to 1947). Oil on canvas, 64×80 cm. Signed bottom right: "Marquet." In S. I. Shchukin collection until 1918; then in the Museum for Modern Western European Art from which it was acquired in 1948. Like many others of his views of Paris, this work was painted from the window of the artist's studio. By improving the expressiveness of the Fauvists' shades of color, Marquet created the modern type of urban landscape.

117 *Fishing boats*. André Derain (1880–1954). Oil on canvas, 82×101 cm. Signed bottom right: "A. Derain." In I. A. Morozov collection in Moscow until 1918; then in the Museum for Modern Western European Art from which it was acquired in 1948. This painting is from the artist's Fauvist period, when he was applying the techniques of neo-Impressionist pointillism and making his colors increasingly luminous.

118 *View from the window*, 1913. André Derain. Oil on canvas, 128×79 cm. Signed on the back of the canvas: "A. Derain." In S. I. Shchukin collection until 1918; then in the Museum for Modern Western European Art from which it was acquired in 1948. Derain went through Fauvist and Cubist periods and inclined toward neo-Primitivism, drawing ideas from old Italian and Dutch art. His figures had a marked linear character, and his colors were expressive and harsh.

119 *Portrait of the writer Sabartés*, 1901. Pablo Picasso (1881–1973). Oil on canvas, 81×66 cm. Signed top left: "Picasso." In S. I. Shchukin collection until 1918; then in the Museum for Modern Western European Art from which it was acquired in 1948. The Spanish writer, D. Sabartés (1881–1968) was a childhood friend of Picasso's. In 1946 he published his memoirs about the artist. The painting is from Picasso's Blue Period (1901–1904).

120 *Acrobat on a ball*, 1905. Pablo Picasso. Oil on canvas, 146×94 cm. Signed bottom right: "Picasso." In I. A. Morozov collection until 1918; then in the Museum for Modern Western European Art from which it was acquired in 1948. *Acrobat on a ball* is a masterpiece of Picasso's Pink Period (1905–06). The painting belongs to a series on circus artists. For a while it belonged to the American writer, Gertrude Stein, who also sat for Picasso on a number of occasions.

121 *Pine trees: Saint-Tropez*, 1909. Paul Signac (1863–1935). Oil on canvas, 72×92 cm. Signed bottom right: "P. Signac 1909." In S. I. Shchukin collection until 1918; then in the Museum for Modern Western European Art from which it was acquired in 1948. From 1892 on, Signac lived mostly in Saint-Tropez, a small town on the French Mediterranean coast. The works he painted there depict the sea and coastal scenery in a strict pointillist style. This painting is an early example of the move away from pure neo-Impressionism in the style of Georges Seurat. With inspiration from the Fauvists, the strokes in Signac's painting became softer and his colors brighter.

122 *Muse inspiring the poet*, 1909. Henri Rousseau (1844–1910). Oil on canvas, 131×97 cm. Signed bottom right: "H. Rousseau. 1909." In S. I. Shchukin collection until 1918; then in the Museum for Modern Western European Art from which it was acquired in 1948. The painting depicts the famous French poet,

Guillaume Apollinaire (1880–1918), and the painter, Marie Laurencin (1885–1956). This double portrait glorifies the poet, who was a friend of Rousseau's. A variation of this painting can be found in Basle.

123 *Eve.* Auguste Rodin (1840–1917). Marble, height 76 cm. Signed: "Rodin." In M. A. Morozov collection until 1903; then in the Museum for Modern Western European Art from which it was acquired in 1948. This statue illustrates the mastery of the French sculptor in the treatment of both form and material.

124 *The river nymph.* Claude Michel Clodion (1738–1814). Terra cotta, height 25 cm. Acquired in 1928 from Bras collection in Leningrad. Clodion reached his peak in the 1770s and 1780s. This famous master of small sculpture is represented here by a typical work in rococo style.

125 *Building workers,* 1951. Fernand Léger (1881–1955). Oil on canvas, 160×220 cm. Signed bottom right: "51 F. Léger." This painting belongs to the *Builders* cycle, which Léger worked on in 1950–51. The painter was interested at that time in the problems of workers and technology. The painting is in Léger's characteristic color combination of red, black, and white.

MUSEUMS OF THE MOSCOW KREMLIN

A fortress in ancient times, the Kremlin today is a distillation of Moscow history, past and present. Within its walls is the largest aggregation of museums in Moscow. Important collections are housed in buildings of unparalleled architectural beauty: the State Armory, which is the oldest Russian museum, the Cathedral of the Annunciation, the Cathedral of the Assumption, the Cathedral of Michael the Archangel, and the Church of the Deposition of the Robe.

THE STATE ARMORY

The Armory was first mentioned in the sixteenth century as a place for storing weapons. The largest workshop of the period, it flourished in the middle of the seventeenth century when it produced armor, cutting weapons, and firearms. In those days it was situated near the Troitski Gate, together with other workshops, such as the State Treasure Court, the treasure house for equestrian armor, and the chamber for vestments and linen. Chronicles of the seventeenth century record the existence of the Gold and Silver Chamber, the Chamber of Sacred Articles, and the Icon Chamber.

Gradually some of the chambers were closed or restricted in their usage. In the 1670s the Icon Chamber became simply the icon workshop. In 1683, the first Russian workshop for secular painting was established; here famous artists such as Ushakov and Pavlovets, who had received the title "Painter for the Tsar," were employed. In 1700, the Gold and Silver Chamber was incorporated into the Armory, and from then on jewels and precious garments were kept there.

In the seventeenth century the Kremlin workshops constituted a kind of art academy in which traditional crafts were practiced. By the beginning of the eigh-

teenth century, however, production had decreased drastically; costly weapons were rarely made in the Armory workshops, and master craftsmen had little to do. In 1711, under Peter I, the greater part of the workshop was moved to St. Petersburg. The Armory was now primarily a storage place for works of art and craftsmanship with only minor workshops for maintenance and preservation—the first step toward its future role as a museum. In 1720, Peter I designated the Armory as the treasure house of the tsar's family. By 1727 the Kremlin's various workshops and storerooms were fully integrated into a combined workshop and armory.

It was not until well into the eighteenth century that an attempt was made to classify the collections and turn the Armory into a museum. This was the task of the first president of Moscow University, A. Argamakov, who was instructed to examine the Armory and its contents. As soon as he saw how little classifying had been done, he suggested that an inventory be made, a catalogue printed, and a building constructed especially to house the collections. He also requested a visitors' day once a week. The senate acknowledged the need for a new building and for an inventory of the collections and commissioned the architect, D. Ukhtomsky, to design the building. In 1756, construction was begun on stone galleries on the site of the former Treasure Court next to the Cathedral of the Annunciation. The work dragged on for several years; in the end the collections were not transferred, and the building was never used as a museum. The Armory remained a Court museum, and was accessible only to a limited number of visitors. Toward the end of 1768 Catherine II ordered demolition of the building as it hampered construction of the Great Kremlin Palace. Some of the Armory's treasures were moved to St. Petersburg; the remainder were stored in damp cellars. In 1792 a number of particularly valuable items was placed in the Palace of Facets in the Kremlin.

A turning point for the Kremlin's collections finally came at the beginning of the nineteenth century with the foundation in 1804 of the Society for Russian History and Antiquities at Moscow University. Its aim of transforming the Armory into a national museum gained ground, especially under the leadership of P. S. Valuyev. In 1806, the tsar issued a decree on the administration and proper storage of the collections in the antiquities workshops and in the Armory. The decree embodied an order to prepare and print an "Historical Description of the Kremlin," with drawings and tables, and provided for a budget and research. The Armory was finally and officially recognized as a museum.

Between 1806 and 1812 a new building, designed by the architect, I. V. Yegotov, rose on the site of the former palace of Boris Godunov. Napoleon's invasion of Russia prevented the treasures from being moved into their new home immediately; instead they were hidden in Nizhny-Novgorod. It was not until 1814 that the treasures were put on display in the museum's seven halls. The building, adorned with sculptures of generals and other famous people of the past, was magnificent, but it proved to be unsuitable as a museum. In 1851, construction of the present museum, designed by the architect, K. A. Thon, and located near the Borovitski Gate, was finished.

Until the Russian Revolution of 1917, the Armory remained virtually a Romanov family museum, true to Peter I's decree that it should be a treasure house for the possessions of the tsar's family. Only after the Revolution did the Kremlin collections become state property and thus accessible to the whole nation.

After 1918 new exhibits were added to the Armory from former royal property, from the patriarchs' sacristy, and from cathedrals and churches. Through large-scale scientific classification, the museum's treasures were finally arranged according to historical and artistic value, genre and technique, and time and place of creation. The year 1920 saw the first special exhibitions—on weaving and enameling. In 1924, the first showing of the permanent exhibits was held. During the Second World War, the museum's treasures were moved to the country for safety; they were returned and the museum reopened in 1955.

Today the Armory's many sections offer the viewer a wide assortment of riches. The eight thousand items in the collection of military and ceremonial weaponry include cutting weapons and firearms made between the thirteenth and nineteenth centuries in various countries (Russia, Byzantium, Montenegro, Iran, Turkey, Egypt, India, and Germany). Among the items on display are helmets, chain mail, shields, axes, hunting spears, swords, sabers, arrows, and military spears. A large collection of small arms is highlighted by weapons that used to belong to famous generals and other heroes.

The collection of Byzantine jewelry and small sculptures bears witness to the bustling trade between Russia and Byzantium between the fifth and fifteenth centuries. It also demonstrates the way Byzantine masterpieces influenced Russian and medieval art.

The collection of Russian gold and silver from the twelfth to seventeenth centuries has excellent examples of various techniques, such as embossed work, niello, engraving, colored enameling, and gem cutting. Most of the articles were made by Muscovite masters of the sixteenth and seventeenth centuries, but works from other centers of applied art (Yaroslavl, Novgorod, and Zolvychegorsk) are also on display. A smaller collection of works from earlier centuries has also been preserved.

Russian gold and silver pieces from the eighteenth and nineteenth centuries in rococo and classical styles are the work of skilled craftsmen from Moscow, St. Petersburg, Veliky Ustyug, and Vologda.

The Western European silver collection covers the thirteenth to nineteenth centuries and comprises art works by masters from England, Switzerland, Germany, France, Denmark, and Holland. There are numerous fine examples of the work of German silversmiths in such centers as Nuremberg, Augsburg, and Hamburg. Most of these objects were acquired in 1628 when the treasures of the Danish king, Christian IV, were put up for sale. Periods represented include the fifteenth and sixteenth centuries, Gothic and Renaissance.

The collection of Russian, Oriental, and European precious fabrics of the fourteenth to eighteenth centuries contains satin, silk, silk/velvet, and velvet embroidered in gold and studded with pearls and precious stones. Vestments of high ecclesiastical dignitaries are preserved here, together with Gobelins by Russian and foreign craftsmen. Some of the oldest materials date back to the fourteenth century. There are some superb garments made of Oriental silk (sixteenth century) and of Italian velvet (seventeenth century), ceremonial robes of Russian tsarinas, and a survey of the development of Russian and Western European fashion of the eighteenth and nineteenth centuries. One section of the museum is devoted to a fascinating collection of old royal regalia, including thrones, scepters, and imperial orbs and crowns, richly encrusted with precious stones.

Another intriguing section displays a collection of old carriages and exotic harnesses. The French coaches, often decorated by famous painters like Boucher, are particularly distinctive.

These sections represent only a sampling of the Armory's treasures. The museum also has collections of glass, porcelain, stone, bone, mother of pearl, and rare woods; flags, orders of distinction, watches and clocks, and tobacco boxes; and 'the world's largest historic collection of gifts from foreign diplomats.

THE CATHEDRAL
OF THE ANNUNCIATION

The Cathedral of the Annunciation (Blagoveshchenski Sobor) was built under Ivan III between 1484 and 1489 on the foundations of a fourteenth-century church. The builders were from Pskov, but the cathedral's architecture is in true Moscow style. In 1564 it was rebuilt—the original three cupolas were replaced by five domes, and open passageways were transformed into a gallery. The cathedral is connected to the palaces by galleries.

Today the Cathedral of the Annunciation is a treasure house of ancient Russian painting. The icons belonged to the original church, and were later moved to the new cathedral. The Deësis row of the iconostasis includes eleven icons by Theophanes the Greek (for example, Christ Pantocrator, Virgin Mary, John the Baptist, Apostle Peter); the others were painted by Andrei Rublyov and Prokhov from Gorodets. Seven of the fifteen icons on the third tier are attributed to Rublyov; the remainder date from the sixteenth century. The icons of the prophets on the fourth tier were painted in the sixteenth century, and those of the Early Fathers on the last tier nearly all originated in the nineteenth century. The design of the high form of iconostasis evolved in Byzantium, but was perfected in ancient Russian art. The one in the Cathedral of the Annunciation is characteristic.

Sixteenth-century frescoes decorate the walls of the cathedral. Most of the substantial collection of icons in the south gallery had been an integral part of the cathedral; the others were transferred from other collections in the Moscow Kremlin.

THE CHURCH OF THE
DEPOSITION OF THE ROBE

Built in 1484–85 by masons from Pskov on the site of a church that had burned down in 1473, the Church of the Deposition of the Robe (Tserkov Rizpolozheniya) is situated behind the Cathedral of the Assumption. This fairly small church is similar to the Cathedral of the Assumption but, in contrast to it, has one dome. The façades of the church are adorned with terra-cotta figures and the three apses with arcatures. On the southern façade, a fifteenth-century portal, consisting of half and quarter pillars, one above the other, has survived. When Metropolitan Nikon built a new palace in the seventeenth century, the church became the palace church. Its interior was connected to the tsar's chambers in the Terem Palace. In 1644, S. Osipov and I. Borisov decorated the walls and vaults with frescoes, which were restored a few decades ago. In the eighteenth and nineteenth centuries, chapels were built onto the church.

In 1965 the church was opened as a museum. Old Russian wooden sculptures and figures, mostly by seventeenth-century Muscovite wood carvers, are on display in the gallery. Numerous carvings were destroyed in the eighteenth and nineteenth centuries after a decree ordered the removal of sculptures from the cathedrals. Because only a few examples of the old Russian art of wood carving remain, special attention has been paid recently to ensure their preservation. An expressive folklore style and bright colors are typical of these old Russian carvings.

THE CATHEDRAL
OF MICHAEL THE ARCHANGEL

In 1505, Ivan III commissioned the Italian architect, Alevisio Novi, who had arrived in Moscow the year before, to build a new church on the site of the dilapidated, old Cathedral of Michael the Archangel (Arkhangelsky Sobor). Modeled on the Cathedral of the Assumption, the new building was to serve as a mausoleum for the capital. It was finished in 1508.

The cruciform-domed basilica with six pillars has a wide nave and transept, which form a large area at the point where they cross. Decorative features of the cathedral are the characteristic pilasters crowned with capitals and fluted niches in each section of the façade. The walls of the vestibule at the west portal are adorned with frescoes. Originally a gallery surrounded the cathedral on the north, south, and west sides. Little light can penetrate into the cathedral, as in the seventeenth century the windows on the south side were walled up. Inside the cathedral are 46 sarcophagi of Russian princes and tsars of the fifteenth to eighteenth centuries.

Praying to one's deceased ancestors was an extremely important ceremony in this mausoleum, as the murals illustrate. The frescoes that have survived to this day date from the period 1652–1666. They were painted by famous artists from the Armory, such as Rezanets, Y. Rudakov, Ushakov, and F. Subov. The iconography and themes of the paintings show that they were modeled on examples of old frescoes from the sixteenth century, probably those from the old cathedral, which were painted by Theophanes the Greek. The frescoes contain many images of Russian princes and tsars, glorifying the rulers of the state. Idealized portraits depict Byzantine emperors (to document the succession of the Christianizing state) and princes who have been elevated to sainthood. The paintings on the south and north walls are devoted to the life of Michael the Archangel, the west wall is covered by a painting of the Last Judgment.

THE CATHEDRAL OF THE ASSUMPTION

The Cathedral of the Assumption (Uspensky Sobor) is the largest building in the Kremlin. It is the fifth building constructed on this site since the original twelfth-century wooden church. Its immediate predecessor caved in before it was even finished.

Russian princes and tsars showed interest in the construction of the Cathedral of the Assumption because it was to be the main church of Moscow and later of the whole Moscow principality.

Ivan III decided to recruit Venetian masters to build the cathedral. On his behalf, the Russian ambassador, S. Tolbuzin, engaged the famous architect and engineer, Aristotle Fioravanti, who arrived in Moscow in 1475. He persuaded Ivan III to demolish the collapsed building and start afresh. Fioravanti went to Vladimir in order to study old Russian architecture and examined the old Cathedral of the Assumption there which had been suggested as a model. In 1479 the new building was completed and officially consecrated.

The architectural style of the building indeed has much in common with the Cathedral of the Assumption in Vladimir, but it also displays some novel features. These include regularity and symmetry—an expression of the creator's admiration for the Renaissance. Fioravanti constructed a building that is impressive in its solemn and monumental character. The design of the interior was also unusual, astonishing people of the time by its size. Tall, strong columns support the vaults, and there is none of the traditional galleries. The columns were originally crowned by capitals, but these were knocked off during restoration work at the beginning of the seventeenth century. Since the nineteenth century the floor has been covered by square slabs of cast iron.

In 1481, the painter, Dionisi, and his assistants Timofei, Yarets, and Konya, produced a three-tiered iconostasis. It appears originally to have been a low, stone barrier adorned with frescoes and icons. The present iconostasis was made in the mid seventeenth century and consists of five tiers. In the 1840s it was restored and covered in chased silver gilt. Some of the icons were painted over.

The interior walls were covered with frescoes, which between 1642 and 1644 were painted over. Additional touch-ups were frequent in subsequent years, further hiding the originals. The first attempts at restoration began in 1911 after surviving fragments of the original paintings from the end of the fifteenth and beginning of the sixteenth centuries had been discovered. Systematic restoration of the frescoes only started properly in 1960. In certain places, the seventeenth-century overpainting was preserved, as it was the work of well-known artists such as B. Savin, I. Paissein, Osipov, and M. Matveyev. The frescoes on the cathedral walls depict scenes from the life of Mary and the Early Fathers.

Saint George and *Our Lady of Vladimir,* now in the Tretyakov Gallery, used to be kept here. The cathedral also has a number of interesting examples of applied art—the door to the south portal, the throne of Ivan the Terrible, and the patriarch's shrine. The chandeliers date from the seventeenth century.

NOTES ON ILLUSTRATIONS

THE STATE ARMORY

126 *Crown of Monomakh,* late 13th to early 14th century. Gold with precious stones, filigree, pearls, sable. This, the oldest hereditary tsarist crown, is believed to be an example of Oriental workmanship. All Russian tsars before Peter I were crowned with it. There are numerous legends about the crown's origin, the most common being that it was sent to the Kiev Prince Vladimir Monomakh from the Byzantine Emperor Constantine Monomachus. This legend is widely believed because it acknowledges the Byzantine line of succession of Russian princes and tsars. The upper part of the crown consists of eight longish lamellae with exquisite filigree ornamentation. A gold cap rises above the lamellae and finishes in a smooth gold cross with pearls. This headpiece as well as the precious stones—rubies and emeralds—are additions of the sixteenth century. The crown is edged in sable.

127 *Helmet,* late 12th to early 13th century. Silversmith's work. This is the oldest warrior helmet in the collection. It was found in 1808 by the river Kloksha near Yuryev-Polski. In 1843, A. N. Olyonin, president of the Academy of Arts, presented it to the museum. The helmet bears clear signs of its age, being rusty and with parts missing. It is in the form of a bolt, forged out of a single sheet of metal. The embossed silver edge on the lower part is embellished with acanthus leaves, birds, and griffins. The front part of the helmet bears embossed work depicting Michael the Archangel, the leader of the heavenly armies and the patron of commanders. There are four silver panels around the pointed upper part of the helmet—with relief portraits of Christ and the saints Feodor, George, and Vassily.

128 *Necklets,* 12th century. Ryazan. Filigree, cloisonné enamel, gold with pearls, and precious stones. In 1822, treasure was found near Staraya Ryazan, the former capital of a feudal principality. It was established as having belonged to the family of an archduke, and was buried to keep it from the Tartar and Mongolian invaders. Included in this treasure was a type of heavy necklet consisting of medallions threaded together with pearls and worn over one's clothes. The central link of the necklet has an enamel picture of Mary, and the adjacent medallions depict Saint Irene and Saint Barbara. The last two links do not have enamel pictures, and are adorned only with filigree and jewels.

129 *Sakkos* (sack cloth), 14th to 15th century. Satin, gold embroidery, pearls. "Sakkos" is the old Russian word for a penitential robe. The term was retained for a church vestment in spite of the rich decoration of pearls and jewels. This robe belonged to Archbishop Photius, who became the Metropolitan of Moscow in 1409. The blue satin is embroidered in gold—the work of Byzantine experts. There are pearl-edged crosses and circles on the sakkos, with scenes from the New Testament and portraits of great Moscow princes and of Photius himself embroidered in them. There is an inscription along the edge.

130 *Cover of a gospel,* 1571. Moscow. Gold, enamel, filigree, precious stones. The covers of liturgical books were usually made of silver and gold and adorned with niello, filigree, and jewels. This cover, which was ordered by Ivan the Terrible, was made by masters of the Armory and was presented to the Cathedral of the Assumption in the Kremlin. It is embellished with five round medallions, four of which are placed symmetrically in the corners and contain the figures of the Evangelists. The center medallion depicts the resurrection of Christ. The background is covered with filigree flowers and leaves in enamel. The central part is studded with tourmalines, rubies, sapphires, and other precious stones.

131 *Dish,* 1561. Moscow. Gold, niello. It is believed that this gold dish was made for the wedding of Tsar Ivan IV with Kucheniya, the daughter of the Kabardinian Prince Temryuk, who received the baptismal name of Maria. According to old Russian tradition, wedding jewelry was presented to the brides of distinguished families on a magnificent gold dish. This dish weighs about three kilos. In the center there is a medallion displaying the state coat of arms in niello. The edge is decorated with plant ornamentation in niello with the following inscription: "In the Summer of 1570 this dish was made for the orthodox tsarina, Archduchess Maria, in testimony of the favor of the God-fearing Tsar and Archduke Ivan Vassilyevich, the ruler of all Russia." In 1569, after Maria Temryukovna's death, the dish was given to the Trinity Monastery of St. Sergius (Troitsa-Sergiev-Lavra); it was moved to the Armory in 1928.

132 *Chalice,* 12th century. Pereyaslavl-Zalessky. Gilt, silver, engraved. This chalice was kept in the Monastery of the Saviour in Transfiguration (Spaso-Preobrazhensky monastyr) in Pereyaslavl-Zalessky. According to legend, Prince Yuri Dolgoruky, the founder of Moscow, presented it himself to the monastery. The chalice is wide at the top and has a wide base and a stem with a knob in the shape of an apple. There is an engraved liturgical inscription along the edge of the vessel. It is also engraved with a double line of gilt figures of saints. The base is adorned with broad leaf designs.

133 *Incense vessel,* 1598. Moscow. Gold with precious stones (niello). This incense vessel is one of the best examples of 16th-century niello art. It was commissioned by Tsarina Irina Godunova from the masters of the Armory and, after the death of her husband, Feodor Ivanovich, was given to the Cathedral of the Archangel, together with other treasures. The form of the incense vessel is reminiscent of 16th-century Moscow architecture. It is designed like a small single-domed cathedral with two rows of *kokozhniki* and an onion-shaped roof over a silver tambour, finishing in a cross. The intricate plant ornamentation in niello covers the upper part, which is adorned with sapphires, emeralds, and rubies in raised settings. The eight-leafed base bears an inscription in niello from the donor. Figures of the Apostles appear on one of the sides and two saints on the other—the protectors of the tsar's family. A decree was issued by the Patriarch limiting the incense vessel's use to a maximum of nine times a year.

134 *Helmet,* 1621. Nikita Davydov. Moscow. Iron with gold embossment, pearls, enamel, precious stones. The helmet of Tsar Mikhail Ivanovich Romanov was made by one of the best-

known Russian goldsmiths in the Armory. Of red iron, it is cone-shaped and adorned with gold crowns and fine ornamentation. At the lower edges, rubies and diamonds are mounted in gold, enameled settings. The helmet carries the following inscription in Arabic: "Give joy to believers with the promise of Allah's help and an early victory." It has a long back part covered with panels, ear sections covered with fine gold grass ornamentation, and a damascene nose shield to which a gold coat with the embossed figure of a guardian angel is attached. The traditional Russian embellishment and the Arabic inscriptions combine harmoniously on the gold pattern.

135 *Chalice of Tsarina Irina Godunova,* 1598. Moscow. Gold with niello and precious stones. This chalice was also presented to the Cathedral of the Archangel by Tsarina Irina Godunova. It is adorned from top to bottom with niello and encrusted with precious stones. The Deësis—Christ, Mary, and John the Baptist—is portrayed in medallions in the middle of the chalice. They are reminiscent of masterpieces in paintings of that time. The dark plant ornamentation in niello harmonizes perfectly with the large sapphires and rubies in raised embossed settings.

136 *Bratina,* first half of 17th century. Silver, embossed. The "bratina," a spherically shaped drinking vessel, is an essential part of a festive table. In ancient Russia it was used for toasts and for passing around. This bratina is supported by figurines. The sides are lavishly adorned with embossed plant and animal motifs. A maxim is engraved along the edge in exquisite ornamental writing. The Kanfarenie technique was used to make the silver bratina; that is, to emphasize the embossed work, the base was covered in richly adorned indentations, giving the appearance of a mat surface. The pointed lid of the vessel is crowned by a bouquet of flowers.

137 *Imperial orb and scepter,* mid 17th century. Constantinople. Gold with precious stones. The orb and scepter belonged to Tsar Alexei Mikhailovich. The massive gold orb is embellished with green enamel, rubies, and diamonds. The scepter ends in a Greek cross, flanked by double eagles, symbols of the Tsar's coat of arms.

138 *Dish,* 1653. Moscow. Gold with precious stones and enamel. The dish is hemispherical and stands on a high base. The outside surface is divided into sections by magnificent bouquets of flowers in enamel. The wide border at the edge contains an inscription in black enamel, which states that the dish was a gift from Patriarch Nikon to Tsar Alexei Mikhailovich. Two large sapphires and two emeralds are set in the inscription.

139 *Our Lady of Smolensk,* late 16th century to early 17th century. Moscow. Gold with precious stones, embossed work, niello. The molding on the icon is embellished with sapphires, emeralds, rubies, and tiny panels with scenes in niello. The halo around Mary's crown is of embossed gold. The oldest layer of painting dates from the 15th century.

140 *Goblet in the form of a cock,* 15th century. Silver. The so-called chicken goblet, which belonged to the Moscow prince, Ivan III, is the oldest item in a collection of decorative objects made out of amber, gray marble, crystal, coconut, and ostrich eggs. Made mostly by German craftsmen, they were brought to Russia from various countries between the 15th and 18th centuries.

141 *Boris Godunov's saddle,* early 17th century. In the 16th and 17th centuries, great importance was attached to the tsar's appearance on horseback. The magnificence of the equestrian adornment was very impressive. The shape of the saddle was determined by Russian military tactics. The front part of Russian saddles was raised and tilted forward. Boris Godunov's saddle is ornamented with finely embossed flowers and birds.

142 *Boris Godunov's coach,* late 16th to early 17th century. England. Boris Godunov received this coach in England as a gift. It ranks among the oldest carriages in the Moscow collection and is large, heavy, and simple in structure. The coach body is strapped into place, with no suspension, and there is no coach box. The horse was driven with a bridle or ridden. The coach is fitted with curtains, and the interior contains seats covered in Persian velvet. The coach body is adorned with painting and wood carving, depicting a triumphal procession, a victorious army, and Christians battling against Moslems, as well as scenes of hunts for bears, wild boar, and tigers.

143 *Catherine II's coach,* 1769. England. This scarlet coach for four was built by the English craftsman, Bockindale. It is extremely stable, with vertical and horizontal suspension, cushioning heavy jolts. The body of the coach is decorated with gilded wood carvings, depicting flower garlands and bouquets, and with pastoral paintings by pupils of Watteau. The coach was still used in the 19th century on festive occasions.

THE CATHEDRAL
OF THE ANNUNCIATION

144 *West portal.* The west portal and the north portal served as official entrances from the gallery into the cathedral. The style of both portals was Italian, as were the portals of the Palace of Facets and the Cathedral of the Assumption, which were used as models. They are distinguished by their complicated arabesques and architectural features such as double pillars and archivolts, which were unknown in ancient Russian architecture. The portals appear to have been constructed on the site of older more traditional ones. Local white stone was dyed dark blue, and the ornamentation was gilded.

145 *The Last Judgment,* 1508. This fresco is situated on the west wall of the cathedral. It was painted by Feodossy, son of the famous artist Dionisi. Feodossy worked with assistants from the Volokolamsk Monastery of St. Joseph. At the end of the 19th century the murals were painted over, and certain sections were destroyed. Current restoration work is uncovering the original paintings as far as possible.

146 *Virgil,* 1564. A portrait in the north gallery of the cathedral. Philosophers and poets of ancient times were portrayed on pilasters here: Aristotle, Menander, Ptolemy, Thucydides, Anaxagoras, Plutarch, Homer, and Virgil. The latter holds a scroll in his hands. His headgear is worthy of note.

147 *The Virgin Mary,* 1405. Theophanes the Greek (from around 1350 to the early 15th century). Distemper on wood. The icon from the Deësis on the iconostasis is situated to the left of Christ the Pantocrator. It was discovered by restorers in 1918, and is an example of the mature style of Theophanes the Greek, who

had moved to Moscow from Novgorod. The icon has monumental features that bestow a solemn and imposing character on the figure of the Virgin. The colors are dark (dark and light blue for her clothes), and her face and hands are modeled with light patches. The figure of the Virgin expresses her love of and devotion to Christ.

148 *John the Baptist*, 1405. Theophanes the Greek. Distemper on wood. *John the Baptist* from the Deësis group of the iconostasis stands to the right of Christ the Pantocrator. The color of his clothing is olive. His figure expresses great humility.

149 *Michael the Archangel*, 1405. Andrei Rublyov (about 1370–1430). Distemper on wood. This icon also comes from the Deësis group of the iconostasis. In contrast to the strict style of Theophanes the Greek, the colors here are clear and light; the expressiveness of the silhouette is replaced by plastic form. The archangel is not as tense as the figures of Theophanes the Greek, and his facial features are gentler.

150 *The transfiguration*. Andrei Rublyov. Distemper on wood. An icon from the feast-day group of the iconostasis. It stands out for its luminous colors, which are a combination of greens, reds, and yellows. Jesus, surrounded by an aureole, appears in light-colored clothes on the mountain of Tabor before his Apostles, who have fallen to the ground in front of him. To the right and left of the aureole are the prophet Elias and the Apostle Mark; below them the Apostles Peter, John, and Jacob are depicted.

151 *The Saviour with golden hair*, early 13th century. Distemper on wood. This is an icon from the Vladimir-Suzdal school, which was then the capital of ancient Russia. The name of the icon is taken from the technique used for the hair, painted with fine strokes on a gold background. The clearly aristocratic features show a trace of sorrow. The cross behind the head on the green background appears to be covered in precious stones. The corners of the icon contain medallions with Christ's monogram. Parts of a blessing can be seen along the edges of the icon.

CHURCH OF THE DEPOSITION OF THE ROBE

152 *Interior view.*

153 *Iconostasis.* The iconostasis was restored in 1963 on the basis of
154 old documents. Nineteenth-century details were removed, and the old wooden parts were reconstructed. The original icons have not survived. The first row of paintings and the second row of smaller icons *(pyadenets)* date from the 17th century, and were brought here from other Kremlin cathedrals. The icons from the third (Deësis) tier, the fourth (feast-day) tier, and the fifth (prophet) tier were painted in 1627 in a workshop directed by Nazari Istomin-Savin. The icon frames are silver with small floral decoration. The colors are deep and solemn; the iconography is consistent with ancient Russian art.

155 *Wooden coffin panels.* In the 17th century it was usual to make
156 wooden coffins for the burial of high dignitaries of the Church.
157 The lids were decorated with portraits of the deceased in ceremonial robes and in a preaching posture. The wooden sculptures were usually painted in gold or silver.

CATHEDRAL OF MICHAEL THE ARCHANGEL

158 *Tomb of the tsar's son, Dmitri Ivanovich*, 1638. The remains of the tsar's son were moved from Uglich in 1606. An ornate canopy in white stone was erected over the tomb.

159 *Iconostasis.* The iconostasis was erected on the site of an older
160 altar screen that had been painted in 1680–81. The present iconostasis was made in 1813, as the original was destroyed in a Kremlin fire during Napoleon's siege. It is in the style of late 17th-century Moscow baroque. The icons date from the 15th to 17th centuries and were brought here from various churches. One of the most famous is *Michael the Archangel with illustrations from his life,* which is situated on the first tier of the iconostasis (second icon to the left of the king's door). It is attributed to Andrei Rublyov.

CATHEDRAL OF THE ASSUMPTION

161 *Relief from the throne of Ivan the Terrible*, 1551. The throne is situated near the south portal of the cathedral. It was made at the beginning of Ivan the Terrible's reign. This wooden throne has the form of a rectangular porch over which rises a high tower-like canopy on lavishly decorated pillars. Bas-reliefs adorn the sides of the lower part. They depict scenes from the legend of the Prince of Vladimir and illustrate in detail Vladimir Monomakh's Thracian campaign and the Byzantine emperor receiving the royal insignia. The scene is accompanied by a text which starts on the door to the throne.

162 *Reliquary*, 1625. A shrine for the relics from Christ's tomb was set up in the southwest corner of the cathedral. The shrine of bronze openwork is crowned by a row of *kokozhniki* and a cone-shaped roof. The craftsman, Dmitri Sverchkov, made the lattice. Seventeenth-century paintings have survived in the interior of the shrine. In 1913 the tomb of Patriarch Hermogen was placed inside it.

163 *Saint George*, 12th century. Distemper on wood. The icon was discovered in 1935 when *Our Lady of Smolensk* was being restored. When the back of the Mary icon was being examined, a portrait of Saint George appeared from under several layers of paint. His head and torso are portrayed from the front; one hand rests on his sword, the other holds a lance. His hair is in curls and his eyes are wide open. The saint is wearing armor and a purple cloak. This figure of a knight resembles very much the hero from the song of Igor.

164 *The Saviour with angry eyes*, early 14th century. Distemper on wood. The icon was painted expressly for the Cathedral of the Assumption. Its name refers to the portrayal of the Saviour as a vengeful god. The icon was obviously painted under the influence of 13th-century Byzantine art. The highly expressive color differentiation is worthy of note.

165 *Door panels in the south portal*. The panels, which were moved
166 from Suzdal to the cathedral in 1410, date from the 12th to 13th century. The doors are made of copper and are decorated in gold on a black background. The panels are separated by torii with medallions portraying saints at their intersections. Each panel

contains an apocryphal subject on the theme of Christ appearing on Earth and the adoration of Christ.

167 *The forty martyrs of Sebaste*, 1481–1515. This fresco is situated on the wall of the Petropavlov predella in the cathedral. Only a fragment showing 24 figures has remained, as part of the wall was removed in 1819 when the tomb of Metropolitan Peter was erected. Presumably the fresco was painted at the same time as other murals commissioned by Archbishop Vassian from Rostov. The style of the fragment is in many respects very different from that of other old paintings. The undamaged fragment depicts the forty martyrs of Sebaste who were sentenced to plunge into ice-cold water. The artist portrays half-naked, suffering people, ready to endure martyrdom.

168 *Metropolitan Peter with scenes from his life*, late 15th to early 16th century. Dionisi. Distemper on wood. Most experts attribute this icon to the artist Dionisi. It is a pendant to the icon *Metropolitan Alexei with scenes from his life* (Tretyakov Gallery). Both icons were commissioned by Ivan Kalita for the Cathedral of the Assumption. After his death, Metropolitan Peter was canonized and revered as the patron of the young Moscow state. The Metropolitan is portrayed with his hand raised to give a blessing. He wears a ceremonial priest's robe in brocade. The figure of the Metropolitan is surrounded by small square scenes depicting the most important events of his life: birth, entry into the monastery, occupation with icon painting, nomination to the throne of the Metropolitan of Galicia, journey to Constantinople, move to Moscow, laying the foundation stone of the Cathedral of the Assumption, interpreting Ivan Kalita's dream, death, burial, and the miracle at the tomb.

169 *Our Lady Bogolyubskaya with scenes from the lives of Sossima and Sabbatios*, 1545. Distemper on wood. This icon is accurately dated, as the painter included the date in the inscription that frames the middle section. It is one of the "northern paintings" of ancient Russian art which was developing at this time under the influence of Muscovite art. It is also notable for the simplicity of its artistic effects and its vivid, folklore elements. The scene depicts the Virgin appearing to the two priests Sossima and Sabbatios—the founders of the Zolovetsky Monastery on the island where the monastery stands. Some of the churches portrayed can be identified exactly. The iconography follows the Moscow style and tradition. The Virgin is protecting the saints and the Russian people. The history of the monastery on the island in the White Sea is illustrated in 33 scenes.

170 *The Assumption*, late 15th to early 16th century. Distemper on wood. This icon was painted for the new Cathedral of the Assumption by contemporaries of Dionisi. The scene in which last respects are being paid to the Virgin is very solemn. Her body is laid out in state. Apostles, priests, angels, and a group of women take part in the ritual. The composition unfolds from the bottom upward. Apostles and angels prepare to give the soul of the Virgin a ceremonious reception in Heaven.

ANDREI RUBLYOV MUSEUM OF ANCIENT RUSSIAN ART

Andrei Rublyov (*c.* 1370–1430) was among the collaborators and immediate followers of Theophanes the Greek. He created distinctive new forms of spiritual expression.

One of the newest museums in the USSR, the Andrei Rublyov Museum of Ancient Russian Art, was opened in 1960 in honor of the six hundredth anniversary of the Russian painter, Andrei Rublyov. The museum is located in the former Andronikov Monastery (Spaso-Andronikov monastyr).

A significant part of Rublyov's life was linked with this monastery. One of the oldest Moscow churches, the early fifteenth-century Cathedral of the Redeemer, stands in the middle of the monastery grounds. Here survive some fragments of murals believed to be the work of Rublyov.

The icons in the monastery museum were collected from the oldest towns and villages around Moscow, Yaroslavl, Kalinin, and Kirov. There are some masterpieces of fifteenth- to sixteenth-century Russian art among them. Newly found works, bearing witness to the diversity of ancient art in Russia, are continually being added to the collection. Skilled technicians work hard to remove layers of overpainting from the icons and reveal the original paintings. In addition to originals, the museum also has copies of frescoes by famous medieval artists of Russia.

The Rublyov Museum often holds special exhibitions and symposia on ancient Russian art. In 1960, it was a new type of museum for Moscow, an experiment, in a way, that has already proved its value. Thanks to this museum, the public has been provided with a representative survey of fifteenth- to seventeenth-century icon painting.

NOTES ON ILLUSTRATIONS

171 *Cosmus and Damianus,* first half of the 15th century. Acquired in 1958; formerly in Pyatnitski Church in the town of Dmitrov. This icon, the work of Muscovite artists, shows the two brothers, who were skilled in medicine and greatly revered in Moscow. Cosmus and Damianus hold their characteristic ointment pots in their hands. The figures of the saints are portrayed from the front. The icon is painted in rich colors and with strong outlines. The stage-like background is in two shades of green, thus giving a sense of perspective.

172 *John the Baptist,* first half of the 15th century. Distemper on wood. Acquired in 1958; formerly in Nikolo Peshnovski Monastery. This icon was done by artists who worked with Andrei Rublyov. It consists of a half-length portrait of the prophet. The gesture of his hand leads the eye to a picture of Christ on the left as though John the Baptist were announcing his coming. The icon is part of the Deësis group of the iconostasis. The monumental quality of form is a feature of Andrei Rublyov's school.

173 *The Apostle Paul,* second half of the 15th century. Distemper on wood. Acquired in 1963; formerly in the village of Chamerovo in the region around Kalinin. This icon is part of the Deësis group of the iconostasis and belongs to the Tversk school. Certain stylistic features point to Andrei Rublyov's style, although expression is emphasized in the portrayal of the face, and linear composition is dominant in the treatment of his clothes. The bible in the hands of the Apostle is shown in reversed perspective.

174 *The Assumption,* last quarter of the 15th century. Distemper on wood. Acquired in 1958; formerly in the Cathedral of the Assumption in the town of Dmitrov. This work was probably painted in Dionisi's workshop. It is a reproduction of the icon of the same name in the Cathedral of the Assumption in the Moscow Kremlin. The diversity of detail, the wealth of poses, and the subtlety of the coloring ushered in a new era in the development of icon painting after Andrei Rublyov's death.

175 *Our Lady Hodegetria,* mid 15th century. Distemper on wood. Acquired in 1958; formerly in the Cathedral of the Assumption in the town of Dmitrov. This icon is the work of Moscow artists.

It corresponds to the basic, developed iconographic representation of the Virgin common in Moscow. The Christ child sits on the Virgin's arm as if on a throne. The round medallions in the top corners contain winged angels praying to the Virgin and Child.

176 *John the Baptist*, mid 16th century. Distemper on wood. Acquired in 1958; formerly in Makhrishski Trinity Monastery near the town of Alexandrov. This icon belongs to the Moscow school. Linked with the tempestuous renewal of iconography in the 16th century, it represents a rare iconographic category. John the Baptist is depicted here as an angel, blessing with one hand and holding a vessel with a severed head in the other (a reference to his agonizing death). At his feet stands a small tree, the top of which has been chopped off with a hatchet—again an indication of the saint's fate. The scroll recounts the story of the saint.

177 *John the Baptist,* mid 16th century. Distemper on wood. Acquired in 1958; formerly in the Cathedral of the Assumption in the town of Dmitrov. This icon belongs to the Moscow school. John

is not portrayed here as a philosopher or an ascetic but as a prophet. His face is deeply lined, betraying immense inner energy. It is framed by stylized brown locks. John the Baptist's pale yellow face stands out clearly against the green background. This figure is painted with great dramatic effect. The icon probably comes from the Deësis group of the iconostasis.

178 *Saint George with scenes from his life*, late 15th to early 16th century. Distemper on wood. Acquired in 1958; formerly in the Pyatnitski Church in the town of Dmitrov. This icon belongs to the Moscow school. In the middle, St. George is portrayed as a knight defending the Kingdom of Heaven against the power of Satan. The cult of St. George was very widespread in ancient Russian art, a fact that undoubtedly can be linked with the struggle against the Mongols who were regarded as heathens. The 16 scenes surrounding the center illustrate the saint's life, his suffering, and his redemption.

HISTORIC ESTATES

Arkhangelskoye Palace Museum
The State Museum of Ceramics in Kuskovo Palace
Ostankino Palace Museum

ARKHANGELSKOYE

Arkhangelskoye is situated in a Moscow suburb. In 1646, the mansion was named after the Church of Michael the Archangel (not to be confused with the Kremlin cathedral of the same name), which was being built on the estate of Prince A. I. Upolotsky. In the latter half of the seventeenth century, the property was taken over by the Odoyevsky family, which was later related to the Golitsyns by marriage. In 1703, Arkhangelskoye was inhabited by Prince D. M. Golitsyn, a supporter of Peter I. He was educated abroad, and traveled extensively in France, Italy, and Germany. His impressions of Western Europe influenced him to have Arkhangelskoye redesigned as a country residence set in parkland. Construction was interrupted in 1736 when Tsarina Anna Ivanovna ordered Golitsyn's arrest and confiscation of his property, including the estate. Golitsyn himself was placed in the fortress, Schlüsselburg, where he died.

Forty years elapsed before his grandson, N. A. Golitsyn, managed to win back the family estate. He then began reconstruction, with the French architect, Charles de Guerne, in charge. The park, containing over fifty statues, was designed by the Italian, Giacomo Trombaro. The design of two pavilions, "Rotunda" and "Caprice," and the library was by serf architects.

The buildings were not all finished when N. A. Golitsyn died, and his widow sold the estate to N. B. Yusupov, one of Russia's richest landholders.

Yusupov was in the diplomatic service and bought art works on behalf of Catherine II and Paul I for the Hermitage in St. Petersburg. In the 1770s, he began to build up his own collection, acquiring first a number of paintings by seventeenth-century Dutch and Italian masters and later some by French artists.

In thirty years Yusupov collected over five hundred paintings by French, Italian, Dutch, Flemish, German, and Spanish masters, including Dolci, Tiepolo, Ricci, Lorrain, Vernet, Robert, Rembrandt, Wouwerman, van Dyck, Rubens, and the English artist, Turner. Some of the paintings were bought at auctions and others were commissioned from contemporary artists, such as Elisabeth Vigée-Lebrun, David, Fragonard, Angelika Kauffman, and Guérin.

Yusupov set up a gallery for his collection in his St. Petersburg residence on the bank of the Fontanka and then in his house in Moscow, which he moved to in 1804. He also decided to reconstruct his country residence near Moscow and use it for his collection, which, in addition to the paintings, included collections of sculpture and porcelain and a substantial library. The serf architect, V. Y. Strishanov, together with the well-known Moscow architects, O. I. Beauvais and Y. D. Tyurin, worked on the buildings until their completion in 1812.

The estate was damaged during Napoleon's invasion but was reconstructed after the war under the guidance of leading Moscow architects. The established seats of other nobility were beginning to be neglected and fall into ruin around this time, and Arkhangelskoye astonished everyone with its magnificence. It was like a relic of a by-gone age, evoking the time of Catherine II. Arkhangelskoye even had its own porcelain factory and its own serf painters.

The decline of Arkhangelskoye, however, was inevitable. After N. B. Yusupov's death, his son reduced the amount of money available for maintenance. He sold the botanical garden, the theater and chapel were closed, and the porcelain factory was leased out. As time went on, Arkhangelskoye was deserted. Some of the painting collection was

37

removed to St. Petersburg where a comprehensive catalogue in French was published in 1836. In the mid nineteenth century, under Prince B. N. Yusupov the Younger, works by Corot, Meissonnier, Isabey, and Troyon were added to the collection.

Nationalized after the 1917 Revolution, Arkhangelskoye was opened to the public on May 1, 1919. In the late 1920s the estate buildings were restored, and numerous paintings from the earlier collection were returned. The works are displayed in roughly the same layout as was used at the beginning of the nineteenth century.

The gallery at Arkhangelskoye centers on the Italian, French, and Dutch schools of painting. Important works trace the development of major themes in mythology, history, landscape painting, and portrait painting. It should be emphasized that the collection includes works that have no counterparts in other museums in the USSR, for example, paintings by the Frenchmen, G. F. Doyen, A. Monger, C.-A. van Loo; the Italians, F. Trevisani and J. Amigoni; and the Flemish painter, A. Diepenbeeck. Seventeenth-century Dutch painting is represented by landscapes by van der Neer, J. Bott, K. Dujardin, still lifes by de Heem, and battle scenes by Wouwerman.

The finest group is the Italian, with two large-scale works by the Venetian, Giovanni Battista Tiepolo, *The meeting of Antony and Cleopatra* and *Cleopatra's banquet,* paintings by J. Amigoni, several landscapes by Francesco Tironi, a collection of miniatures of women's heads by Pietro Rotari, and paintings by the leading artist of Italian classicism, Pompeo Batoni.

Arkhangelskoye's collection of French paintings of the eighteenth century to the beginning of the nineteenth century rounds out the collections of masters of this period in other Soviet museums. Here are landscapes by Lorrain and paintings by Boucher, G. Vernet, Robert, Vigée-Lebrun, and J. L. Prévost. The beginning of the nineteenth century is represented by Gérard, E. Seebach, and artists influenced by David.

The theater, built in 1817–18, contains stage decorations by the Italian, Pietro di Gonzaga (1751–1831), a well-known artist who came to Russia in 1792 and lived there for almost forty years. He also designed the theater itself, which was then named after him.

The church at Arkhangelskoye has an exhibition of ancient Russian art and a collection of works by serf artists. Old pottery and glass are on display in one of the pavilions.

THE STATE MUSEUM OF CERAMICS IN KUSKOVO PALACE

Kuskovo Palace started out as a country residence, built in the sixteenth century on the estate of the boyars Sheremetiev. When Field Marshal B. N. Sheremetiev (1652–1719), who had led the battle of Poltava in 1709, retired, he decided to live at his country residence and had it reconstructed to his taste. Several pavilions, the Chinese Tower, the Turkish House, the Temple of Silence, and the Temple of Love, were built in the park. The design of the new complex appears to have been greatly influenced by the country estates around St. Petersburg.

Later, the Field Marshal's son vastly extended the area of the estate by incorporating into it new pieces of land gained through marriage. It was in his time that Kuskovo got its final look.

The first palace at Kuskovo was built in 1751 and reconstructed in 1771. Serf architects directed the construction of Kuskovo in the 1750s and 1760s. The palace, church, and cottages were built around an artificially constructed drainage system. A French-style garden with statues and pavilions was laid out behind the palace.

In the nineteenth century the palace was neglected. The battles of 1812 caused irreparable damage to Kuskovo, and the new owner chose to build a new country residence to which Kuskovo's treasures were transferred.

Kuskovo itself was rebuilt and used by the owner as a guest house and setting for elaborate banquets. The collection placed there was assembled with this in mind. It included rare objects, such as unique editions of books, scientific instruments, oriental curios, and extravagant bric-à-brac. Some but not all of this collection has remained there.

Today Kuskovo has a substantial portrait gallery, containing paintings mainly from the latter half of the eighteenth century. These are mostly family portraits painted by artists from home and abroad. A collection of still lifes from the 1730s and 1740s includes copies of a few Dutch masterpieces.

In 1932, the Moscow Museum of Porcelain and Ceramics was moved to Kuskovo and in 1938 made part of Kuskovo Palace Museum, which had been established in 1919. Its contents mainly come from the former collections of A. V. Morozov and L. K. Zubalov and comprise eighteen thousand pieces from various countries and epochs. Included are sixteenth-century Italian majolica, Chinese porcelain, Meissen ware, eighteenth-century English porcelain, and porcelain from Sèvres (the well-known "Egyptian service," which Napoleon ordered in 1805 as a present for Alexander I), from Russian factories of the eighteenth and nineteenth centuries, and from modern plants of the Soviet Union. Some of the objets d'art are displayed in the Dutch and Italian pavilions.

OSTANKINO PALACE MUSEUM

The Ostankino country estate was first mentioned in the sixteenth century. Its owner was a foreign office official, V. I. Shchelkalov. The estate originally consisted of a house and church, neither of which exists any longer. The end of the seventeenth century saw construction of another church that is still a decorative asset to the complex today.

In the middle of the eighteenth century the estate was taken over by the Sheremetievs, who were so delighted with Kuskovo's reconstruction, they paid little attention to their new acquisition. N. P. Sheremetiev was the first to decide to turn Ostankino into his main residence in the 1790s. This decision led to a great deal of building. Sheremetiev, who had enormous wealth at his disposal, spent great sums of money between 1792 and 1798 on construction of the main palace in the middle of a park adorned with statues. The palace included a theater, art gallery, a room for a coin collection, and a natural history chamber. It was linked to Italian and Egyptian pavilions by covered galleries.

Several architects worked on the design of the palace, which is basically classical in style. The interior design, which is partly Italian and partly Egyptian, is executed mainly in wood (as in Kuskovo) disguised to imitate marble, bronze, alabaster, and other materials. The décor is elaborate, encompassing a wide variety of ideas, including ceiling paintings, stucco embellishment, decorative sculptures, large mirrors, and crystal chandeliers. Wood carvings, by serf artists, are exceptionally beautiful.

The painting collection was put together more or less haphazardly with paintings sent to Ostankino from various other houses and country residences owned by the Sheremetievs.

The family of the serf artist, Argunov, was responsible for the final selection and display of the works which decorated the main hall.

It is difficult to reconstruct the original collection, as many paintings were removed or stolen in the nineteenth century. After the museum's recent restoration, the gallery was expanded by paintings from other Moscow museums. Nevertheless, the Ostankino is still typical of the Moscow collections assembled in the nineteenth century. Today at the Ostankino, one can find paintings by the Italian artists, M. Campidoglio, D. Langetti, and C. Cignani; the French, J. Dughet, van Loo, M. Gérard; the Dutch, A. Palamedesz; and the Austrian, J. Platzer.

A collection of portraits by the Argunov family is exhibited both at Ostankino and Kuskovo. The collection of copperplate engravings contains works by G. Edelinck, G. Audran, N. Delaunay, D. B. Piranesi, and D. Volpato. The rooms are also decorated with sculptures. Most of them are copies of classical works made by eighteenth-century artists. Original sculptures include *Fighting cocks* by A. Canova, *Milon de Crotone* by Falconet, and *Prometheus, torn by the eagle* by F. G. Gordeyev. Most notable among the classical sculptures are the *Head of Aphrodite* (a Roman copy of the 2nd century B. C. of a Greek original of the 4th century B. C.) and the *Little goat* (from Pompeii, 1st century B. C.).

NOTES ON ILLUSTRATIONS

ARKHANGELSKOYE PALACE MUSEUM

179 *Portrait of an unknown woman.* Anthonis van Dyck (1599–1641). Oil on canvas, 205×119 cm. This portrait was painted in London, where the artist had moved in 1632 at the invitation of King Charles I. Like all the paintings in van Dyck's English period, it is an aristocratic portrait, which is notable for the solemn posture of the model and the distinguished dark coloring.

180 *The meeting of Antony and Cleopatra,* 1747. Giovanni Battista Tiepolo. Oil on canvas, 300×630 cm. The painting shows the meeting of the Egyptian Queen Cleopatra with the Roman general, Antony, who was returning victorious from a military campaign. Antony, bewitched by Cleopatra's beauty, solemnly

hands over to her all his trophies: flags, valuable equipment, and prisoners. This painting, together with its pendant, *Cleopatra's banquet,* which hangs in the same hall, were purchased from the artist's son by N. B. Yusupov.

181 *Startled bather.* François Boucher. Oil on canvas, 55×67 cm. One of Boucher's early works, it depicts the popular rococo subject of a startled bather, here dropping a small basket of flowers into the water.

182 *Chandelier,* early 19th century. The golden empire chandelier in the oval hall of the palace is the work of serf craftsmen.

183 *Vase,* about 1820. Porcelain. This vase was manufactured in the porcelain factory on the estate. The articles produced there were never sold, but were exclusively for the owner's use. In 1822, the running of the workshop was assigned to the French painter, A. F. Lambert, who had formerly worked in the Sèvres factory. Paintings and engravings from Prince N. B. Yusupov's collection were often used as models for painting the porcelain. This empire vase is decorated with scenes from the novel *Atala* by Chateaubriand.

THE STATE MUSEUM OF CERAMICS IN KUSKOVO PALACE

184 *Portrait of P. I. Sheremetieva.* Nikolai Argunov (1771 to about 1829). Oil on canvas. P. I. Kovaliova (Shemchugova on stage, 1768–1803) was a talented serf actress at N. P. Sheremetiev's theater. She obtained her freedom in 1798, and was secretly married to N. P. Sheremetiev in 1801. Soon after, however, she died of tuberculosis in St. Petersburg. The portrait of P. I. Sheremetieva with the red shawl was painted in 1801–02 in St. Petersburg, and is one of the three portraits of her painted by N. Argunov.

185 *Portrait of the Kalmuck girl, Anna Nikolayevna,* 1767. Ivan Argunov (1723–1802). Oil on canvas, 62×50 cm. The Kalmuck girl—a pupil of V. A. Sheremetieva's—is an eleven-year-old wearing a red dress trimmed with lace. She holds in her hands an engraving depicting V. A. Sheremetieva. This work was painted by the forefather of the serf dynasty of distinguished painters under Count Sheremetiev.

186 *Dish.* Bernard Palissy (1510–1590). Ceramic. This dish by the Frenchman, B. Palissy, the inventor of transparent colored glazes, leads the section of French ceramics. The artist decorated his faïences with small figures of animals, fish, and birds. The dish is typical of this master's art.

187 *The Egyptian service* (two pieces), 1805. Porcelain. The service was commissioned by Napoleon in 1805 from the factory in Sèvres. Empire style was a close imitation of the Ancient Egyptian style. The service comprises over three hundred pieces, with models by the designers, Denon and Pair. The biscuit porcelain is heavily gilded. Drawings on certain pieces are reminiscent of copperplate engravings. In 1808, Napoleon presented the service to Tsar Alexander I. It was kept in the Armory until 1918.

188 *George service,* about 1780. Porcelain. The service comes from F. Gardner's private factory near Moscow. Around 1780 the factory was executing a number of large commissions, including the so-called "order" services like the *Andrei, George, Vladimir,* and *Alexander Nevski.* The ribbons of the order were incorporated into the decorative design of the porcelain.

189 *Dish from the Yachts service,* about 1780. Porcelain. In the 1780s the imperial factory produced magnificent services, including the *Arabesque, Cabinet, Yusupov,* and *Yachts.* They are all similar in their ornamentation, and each one comprises close to nine hundred pieces.

190 *Dish.* Porcelain. In 1918, the State Porcelain Factory, directed by the painter, S. V. Chekhonin, began to manufacture so-called "propaganda porcelain." Brightly colored, decorative compositions, combined with rallying cries and slogans, are typical of these items.

OSTANKINO PALACE MUSEUM

191 *The blue hall.* This is the central hall in Ostankino Palace. The walls are covered with a blue and gold ornamental material. A wide, coffered, stucco cornice runs along the edge of the ceiling. A special feature of the hall's decoration are the door frames. The classical atlantes hewn out of granite are based on Ancient Egyptian models. The crystal chandelier adorning the hall dates from the 18th century.

192 *Cocks fighting.* Antonio Canova (1754–1822). Marble. This work is from the artist's Venetian period. The pictorial style indicates his future tendency toward rococo. This masterfully sculptured group depicts the cocks in their natural size. The sculpture can be viewed from all angles, each giving a different "action" view.

193 *Little goat,* 1st century B. C. Marble. This sculpture was found during the excavation of Pompeii. The torso is the work of a Roman master; the legs, head, and stand date from the 19th century. The animal is about a quarter its natural size. Similar sculptures can be found in a number of foreign collections.

THE TRETYAKOV GALLERY

1 Andrei Rublyov. *Trinity*, 1422–1427

43

2 Constantinople school. *Our Lady of Vladimir*, early 12th century
3 Russian and Byzantine masters. *Demetrius of Solun*, about 1113

44

45

46

4 Dionisi. *Crucifixion*, 1500
5 Nikita Pavlovets. *Madonna in the garden*, about 1670

6 Novgorod school. *The miracle of Flor and Laurentius*, last quarter of the 15th century
7 D. G. Levitsky. *Portrait of Pavel Nikolaievich Demidov*, 1773

49

8 D. G. Levitsky.
Portrait of Maria Alexeyevna Dyakova, 1778
9 I. P. Argunov. *Portrait of an unknown woman
in Russian national costume*, 1785

50

10   M. Shibanov. *Wedding ceremony*, 1777

11   O. A. Kiprensky. *Portrait of the writer, Alexander Sergeievich Pushkin,*
     1827
12   I. M. Tankov. *Temple feast,* 1784

53

13 K. P. Bryullov. *Self-portrait*, 1848

14 V. A. Tropinin. *Head of a boy*, about 1818

15 M. I. Lebedev.
Avenue in Albano near Rome, 1836

54

55

16   A. G. Venetsianov. *Ploughing: spring*
17   K. P. Bryullov. *The rider*, 1832

18 V. V. Vereshchagin. *The apotheosis of war*, 1871
19 A. A. Ivanov. *The appearance of Christ to the people*, 1837–1857
20 A. K. Savrassov. *The rooks have come*, 1871

21   V. G. Perov. *Portrait of the writer, Fyodor Mikhailovich Dostoyevsky*, 1872

22   I. N. Kramskoi. *Portrait of the writer, Leo Nikolaievich Tolstoy*, 1873

23 V. I. Surikov. *Boyarynya Morozova*, 1887
24 V. I. Surikov. *The morning of the streltsy execution*, 1881
25 V. E. Borisov-Musatov. *Water container*, 1902
26 M. A. Vrubel. *Demon*, 1890

63

27   I. Y. Repin. *Ivan the Terrible and his son, Ivan, on November 16, 1581,* 1885

28   I. Y. Repin. *Portrait of the writer, Leo Nikolaievich Tolstoy,* 1887

29   M. V. Nesterov. *Vision of the young Bartholomew*, 1889–90
30   A. I. Kuindzhy. *Birch grove*, 1879
31   N. N. Ghe. *Golgotha*, 1892

38   K. S. Petrov-Vodkin. *Red horse bathing*, 1912
39   V. A. Serov. *Portrait of I. A. Morozov*, 1910
40   N. S. Goncharova. *Self-portrait with yellow lilies*, 1907

41   Marc Chagall. *Above the town*, 1914
42   S. E. Serebryakova. *Bleaching linen*, 1917
43   K. S. Petrov-Vodkin. *Petrograd Madonna*, 1920

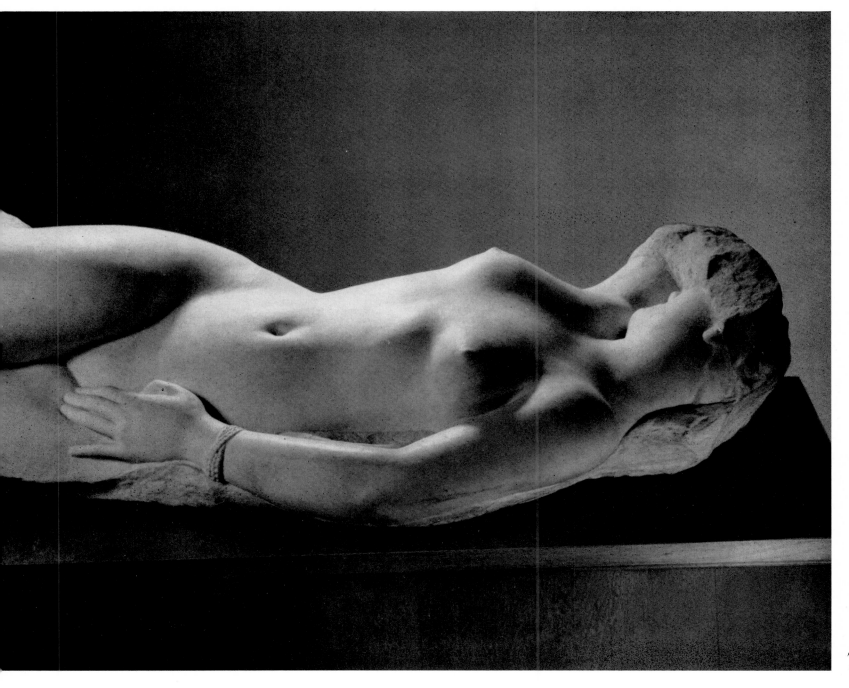

47   I. I. Brodski. *Vladimir Ilyich Lenin in the Smolny Institute*, 1930
48   R. R. Falk. *Red furniture*, 1920
49   A. A. Deineka. *Future pilots*, 1938

50 B. V. Yoganzon. *Interrogation of the communists*, 1933
51 S. A. Chuikov. *A daughter of Soviet Kirghizia*, 1948

81

52   P. P. Konchalovski. *Self-portrait in a yellow shirt*, 1943

THE PUSHKIN FINE ARTS MUSEUM

53   Unknown Faiyum master. *Portrait of a boy with a golden wreath*, early 2nd century A. D.

54 Unknown Byzantine master. *The 12 Apostles*, first half
of the 14th century

55 Giovanni Antonio Boltraffio. *Saint Sebastian*

56   Unknown Italian
master. *Mary enthroned
with the Christ child,*
about 1280

57/58   Stefano di Giovanni (known as Il Sassetta). *Saint Laurentius* and *Saint Stephen*
59   Alessandro di Mariano Filipepi (known as Botticelli). *The Annunciation*

60 Lucas Cranach the Elder. *Mary with the Christ child*

61 Agnolo Tori Bronzino. *The holy family*
62 Dosso Dossi (real name: Giovanni Luteri).
Landscape with scenes from the lives of saints

63   Paolo Caliari (known as Veronese). *Minerva*

64   Bernardo Strozzi. *Coquettish old woman*, 1630

65   Peter Paul Rubens. *Apotheosis of Duchess Isabella*, 1635

66 Peter Paul Rubens. *Bacchanalia,* about 1615

96

97

70 Rembrandt Harmensz van Rijn. *Ahasver, Haman, and Esther*, 1660
71 Rembrandt Harmensz van Rijn. *Portrait of an old woman*, 1654

75   Nicolas Poussin. *Heroic landscape with Hercules*, probably 1665

76   Nicolas Poussin. *Rinaldo and Armida*

104

80   Jean Antoine Watteau. *Bivouac (military camp)*, about 1709–10

81 Alessandro Magnasco. *The nuns' meal*

82   Francesco Guardi. *View of a small Venetian courtyard*

83 François Boucher. *Hercules and Omphale*

84   Jean-Baptiste Pater. *Maypole festival*

85   Jean-Honoré Fragonard. *At the stove*

112

86 Virgilio Narcisso Diaz de la Peña. *The approach of the thunderstorm*, 1871
87 Eugène Delacroix. *After the shipwreck*
88 Jacques-Louis David. *Andromache weeping over Hector*, 1783

113

89　Jules Bastien-Lepage. *True love*, 1882
90　Alfred Sisley. *Frost in Louveciennes*, 1873
91　Pierre Puvis de Chavannes. *Poor fishermen*, 1879

92 Jean-Baptiste Camille Corot. *The gust of wind*
93 Claude Oscar Monet. *Rouen Cathedral at midday*, 1894

117

94 Gustave Courbet. *Mountain hut*
95 Adolph Menzel. *In Luxembourg park*, 1876

96 Jean-François Millet. *Collecting wood*
97 Claude Oscar Monet. *Luncheon on the grass, 1866*

98 Pierre Auguste Renoir. *Portrait of the actress Jeanne Samary*, 1877
99 Pierre Auguste Renoir. *In the garden under trees*, 1875

121

100   Pierre Auguste Renoir. *Nude*, 1876

101   Edgar Degas. *Dancers in blue*, about 1899

102   Paul Cézanne. *Pierrot and Harlequin,* 1888
103   Paul Cézanne. *Peaches and pears*
104   Paul Cézanne. *The plain at the mountain of Sainte-Victoire*

105   Vincent van Gogh. *Red vineyards in Arles*, 1888

106 Vincent van Gogh. *Prisoners' exercise*, 1890

107   Camille Pissarro. *L'Avenue de l'Opéra in Paris*, 1898

108   Henri de Toulouse-Lautrec.
      The singer, Yvette Gilbert, 1894

109   Paul Gauguin. *Café in Arles*, 1888

110   Odilon Redon. *Woman's profile in a window*

111   Maurice Denis. *Polyphem*, 1907

112   Henri Matisse. *The artist's studio*, 1911
113   Henri Matisse. *Goldfish*, 1911

135

117 André Derain. *Fishing boats*
118 André Derain. *View from the window*, 1913

137

119 Pablo Picasso. *Portrait of the writer, Sabartés*, 1901
120 Pablo Picasso. *Acrobat on a ball*, 1905

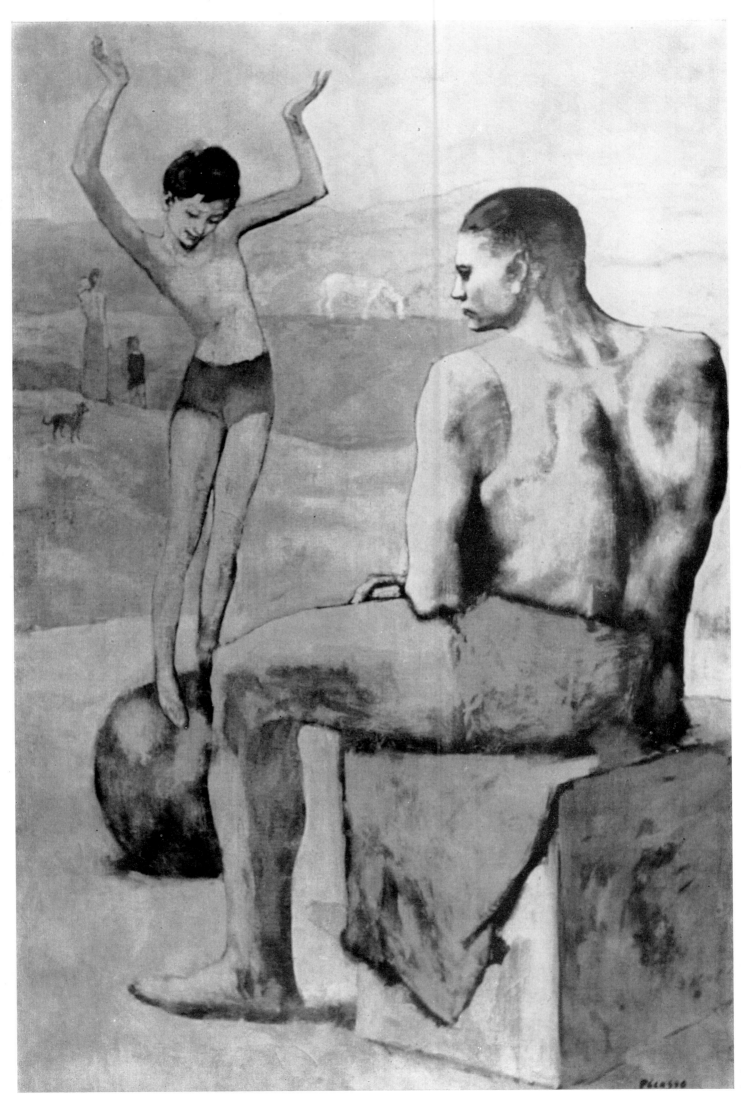

139

121   Paul Signac. *Pine trees: Saint Tropez*, 1909

122   Henri Rousseau. *Muse inspiring the poet*, 1909

143

125　Fernand Léger. *Building workers*, 1951

MUSEUMS OF THE MOSCOW KREMLIN

The State Armory
The Cathedral of the Annunciation
The Church of the Deposition of the Robe
The Cathedral of Michael the Archangel
The Cathedral of the Assumption

126 *Crown of Monomakh*, late 13th to early 14th century

127 *Helmet,* late 12th to early 13th century

128 *Necklets*, 12th century. Ryazan

129 *Sakkos,* 14th to 15th century
130 *Cover of a gospel,* 1571. Moscow

150

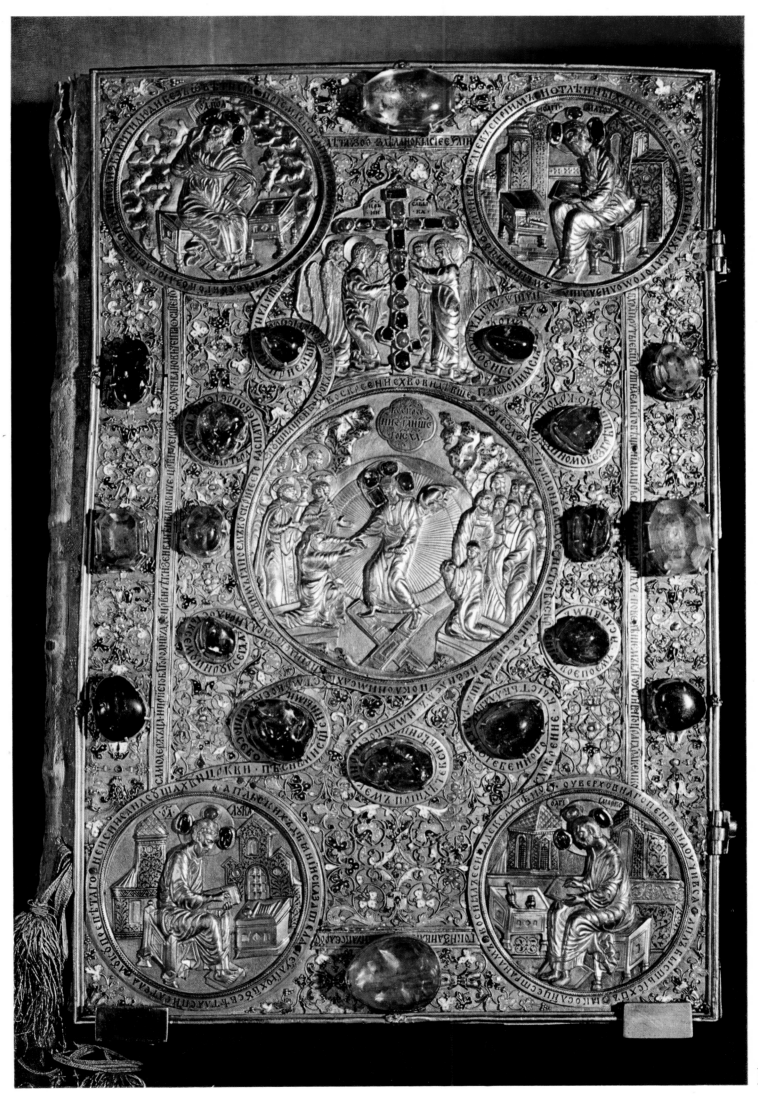

151

131 *Dish*, 1561. Moscow

132 *Chalice*, 12th century.
Pereyaslavl-Zalessky

133 *Incense vessel*, 1598. Moscow

152

153

134 Nikita Davydov. *Helmet*, 1621. Moscow
135 *Chalice of Tsarina Irina Godunova*, 1598. Moscow

155

136 *Bratina,* first half of 17th century
137 *Imperial orb and scepter,* mid 17th century. Constantinople

157

138   *Dish*, 1653. Moscow
139   *Our Lady of Smolensk*, late 16th to early 17th century. Moscow

159

140   *Goblet in the form of a cock*, 15th century

141 *Boris Godunov's saddle,*
early 17th century
142 *Boris Godunov's coach,*
late 16th to early 17th century.
England

143 *Catherine II's coach*, 1769. England
144 *West portal of the Cathedral of the Annunciation*

163

145   *The Last Judgment,* 1508
146   *Virgil,* 1564

147   Theophanes the Greek. *The Virgin Mary*, 1405

148   Theophanes the Greek. *John the Baptist*, 1405

149   Andrei Rublyov. *Michael the Archangel*, 1405

150   Andrei Rublyov. *The transfiguration*
151   *The Saviour with golden hair*, early 13th century

152   *Interior view of the Church of the Deposition*
         of the Robe

153/154   *Iconostasis from the Church of the Deposition*
                of the Robe

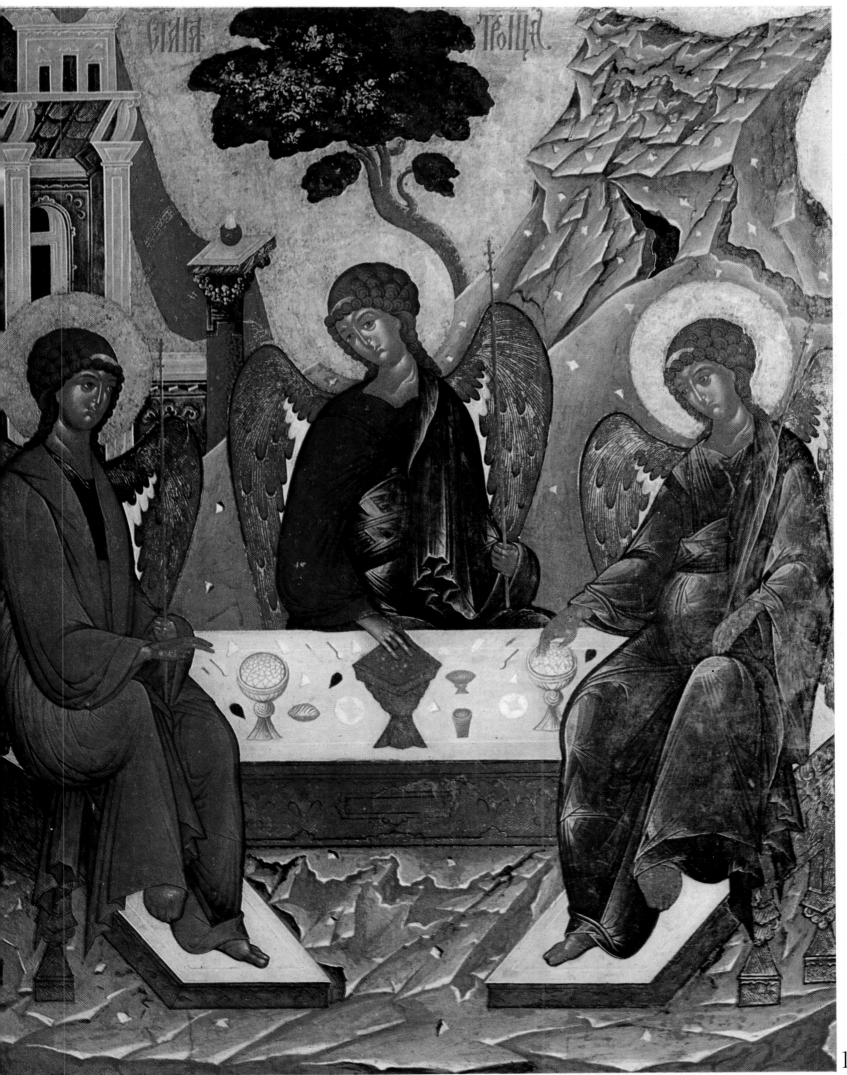

155/156/157 *Wooden coffin panels*
158 *Tomb of the tsar's son, Dmitri Ivanovich, 1638*

159/160   *Iconostasis in the Cathedral of Michael the Archangel*

174

161 *Relief from the throne of Ivan the Terrible,* 1551
162 *Reliquary,* 1625

176

163 *Saint George*, 12th century

178

164   *The Saviour with angry eyes*, early 14th century

165/166   *Door panels in the south portal of the Cathedral of the Assumption*

167   *The forty martyrs of Sebaste*, 1481–1515

168   Dionisi. *Metropolitan Peter with scenes from his life*, late 15th to early 16th century

169   *Our Lady Bogolyubskaya with scenes from the lives of Sossima and Sabbatios*, 1545

183

170   *The Assumption*, late 15th to early 16th century

ANDREI RUBLYOV MUSEUM
OF ANCIENT RUSSIAN ART

171   *Cosmus and Damianus,* first half of the 15th century

172   *John the Baptist,* first half of the 15th century

173   *The Apostle Paul,* second half of the 15th century

174 *The Assumption,* last quarter of the 15th century
175 *Our Lady Hodegetria,* second half of the 15th century

191

192

176　*John the Baptist*, mid 16th century
177　*John the Baptist*, mid 16th century

178 *Saint George with scenes from his life*, late 15th to early 16th century

HISTORIC ESTATES

Arkhangelskoye Palace Museum
The State Museum of Ceramics in Kuskovo Palace
Ostankino Palace Museum

179 Anthonis van Dyck. *Portrait of an unknown woman*

180 Giovanni Battista Tiepolo. *The meeting of Antony and Cleopatra*, 1747

198

181   François Boucher. *Startled bather*

182 *Chandelier*, early 19th century
183 *Vase*, about 1820

200

184   Nikolai Argunov. *Portrait of P. I. Sheremetieva*

185   Ivan Argunov. *Portrait of the Kalmuck girl,*
      Anna Nikolayevna, 1767

186 Bernard Palissy. *Dish*

187 *The Egyptian service*, 1805

188 *George service*, about 1780

189 *Dish from the Yachts service*, about 1780
190 *Dish*
191 *The blue hall of Ostankino Palace Museum*

Gerard de la Barthe pinxit.

Видъ кремлевскаго строенія и его окружности въ Моск...

Иждивеніемъ Іоанна Валзера, Московской Первой Гильдіи Купца Публиковано въ 1799 году съ всевысочайшаго дозволенія ЕГО ИМПЕРАТОРСКАГО ВЕЛИЧЕСТВА ПАВЛА ПЕРВАГО Императора всея Россіи